An Impaired Love

<u>An Impaired Love</u>
&
<u>Love Unimpaired</u>

Written by AJ Ireyes

Copyright 2012, 2014

USA

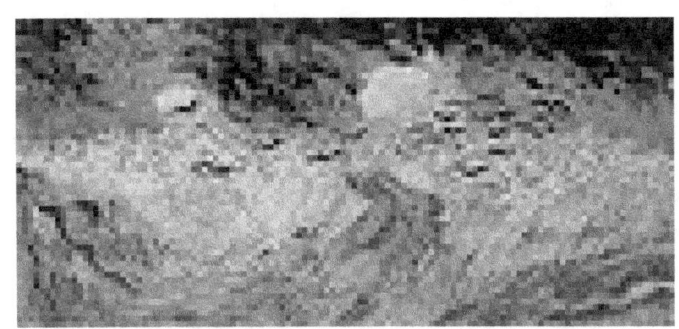

Dedicated to all those who have served.

Contents

AIL

An Impaired Love

&

Love Unimpaired

By AJ Ireyes

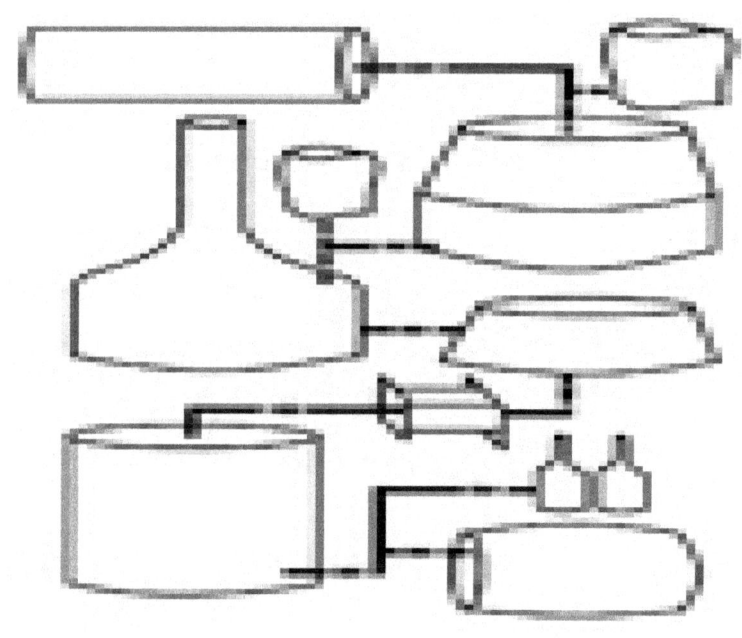

Part I

Ch. 1

That night he left her in tears, but her tears wouldn't change his mind about going through with it, and she said nothing. They tried to make jokes about why Anna wanted a visit so bad, after all they hadn't seen each other in years. Debbie told John to carry his cell phone and to call if he needed her to unknot the ropes from his wrists and ankles when the visit fell through. Debbie felt John had been negligent in accepting the invitation, and had left her home with nothing to occupy her time, but he let out a cliché saying about "doing the right thing" and a line about being punctual. Debbie was taller than him and had a smile that was good for listening to stories, one that made the speaker feel important, but felt her impersonal smile had drawbacks in confrontations with people. She was slender and even in the winter wore light clothes that fell around the curves of her body. Often John would refuse to take her out in the cold afraid she would catch a chill.

After he had left that night in order to arrive early the next morning at Anna's for breakfast,

Debbie knelt over the couch and inhaled the scent that had been left in the hall, the cologne he would wear to work only when he had a meeting after hours. As the scent of caramel and spice dissipated in the foyer she began to cry until she hyperventilated. She heard his car pulling out of the drive and moving away from the house, and it became a bit too much for her to be alone in the place. She had never been alone and away from home with no one to even care for her. John was gone and he had drove off without her so she slept, and when she got up she noticed tears had crept into the corners of her mouth. Tears had burned their way down her face in the night like his scent left at the door had burnt away at her.

For Debbie, knowing he was gone was not enough; instead she needed proof to know just where he had gone. To her he had just left for some faraway place that never had existed. Had he gone home to visit at Anna's request, or was it something he had wanted from Anna. It would only take a full day for John's visit and he would be back in less than twenty-four hours, but Debbie was sorry and worried he would come back differently from when he had left. If he was going back to find the girl he once loved then she was going to be with him somehow. She didn't know why she did it, but Deb went into the room John kept his old personal belongings and memorabilia in and sat on the floor, her knees buried in the carpet as she tried to burn away the image of

Anna and John from her mind like she was lighting a photograph on fire and dropping it in a sink.

There in John's personal room in the early morning Debbie's hyperventilating came back as she tried to speak in some forgotten language that only she could understand. She felt John kneel beside her and speak, but Debbie couldn't make out the words at first, but then slowly she began recognizing the softness in the voice that was telling her it was going to be ok.

She had used her cell phone to call John hoping that it wasn't too late, and that John had not yet reached Anna. Debbie listened at last as John spoke over the phone, "Debbie, calm down. Nothing I'm doing is going to hurt you. You're out of line. Please stop crying!" Debbie tried to keep reasonable and tried to stop the tears, to be safe with her heart, but she believed at moments in life, at least in one moment of life, the heart can break away from the mind and take over; the heart can control the mind and its reasons and actions. She thought the heart when willing rips and tears the images in the mind, it tears them and lights them on fire. Debbie's heart with its thundering, booming, fantastical noise pushed out all the pain and let John see his disappearance, and the guilt it caused, like everyone wants in life.

Debbie told John, "I wanted to see you leave so badly last night just to make you happy, but my heart had no control of my senses and my mind created its own pictures, images, and feelings and all of them of you and her together, all from my guilty senses never wanting to let you go, so I lost control."

Debbie spoke quietly into the cell as she moved through the empty halls of the house, "It is what it takes to keep lonely I suppose- a strong heart and a weak mind." The voice faded off as it spoke soft and slow to Debbie, "I've got to take over for you Debbie, you can't quite tell the truth of the matter." John was in Debbie's heart then and Debbie sat on the lonely leather couch and with her body curled up as tightly as it could be. She wanted John to be close, to be draped around her body so she could feel her lover's warmth. Debbie needed John's arms around her and his hands on her shoulders gently stroking them like he always did when she lost control.

At Anna's the door to the garage opened and the garage inside light came on. Anna appeared in the doorway and saw John as he stood in the doorway in the half light of the early dawn. Under the full incandescent light from within the garage she was beautiful, tall and slender, olive skin, and a round face surrounded by her gorgeous auburn hair. Her weight hadn't changed much, or her complexion, and John agreed now that he had always thought she would look forever the same youthful attractive girl. She gave life to the image in John's head, as he squinted to avoid the flood of man-made light. "Are you all right John? We get into the house through here," She pointed over her shoulder, "the door to the house is just inside here," she said as the smile she carried from before left her.

She John saw too clearly, more clearly than Debbie could at this point, and John could only imagine Anna's reaction as the lights flooded his face and made it tighten just as his eyes began to flicker and adjust. He was having a serious meltdown now in front of Anna, and felt bad as she was the only girl he had trusted in the new city. John was crying and Anna noticed it first by covering her own cheeks with her hands and then by trying to reassure him by coming close to him and pulling at his jacket toward the doorway. As John tried not to give in to her, he fully realized his own wet cheeks and he turned away, his legs gave out underneath him and he cried as he fell to his knees, all he could think of was Debbie.

Anna moved John over to the couch in the center of the room and sat next to him as she leaned back and pushed her side up against him. The room was lit up from the sun outside coming in through the large day window. A large oak waist-high cabinet stood in front of the window and had a white silk fabric draped over the top of it. In the center of the room was a full sized day couch that matched the beige carpet of the house. A tall black vase with aromatic branches stretching out of its top lie in one corner of the room and a lighted ceiling fan was directly overhead of the couch.

But John couldn't see any of this, and he knew he was losing it. He'd of felt better knowing he could gain control of his senses with Anna's assistance, but despite her desperate pleas his own suffered cries grew louder. John's face was pale, and all the color drained from him by the chill of the morning air outside and from his conversation with Debbie on his cell. He had turned off the cell after hanging up with Debbie and now had it in his jacket's interior pocket.

John hadn't known how to handle the situation of Anna seeing him like this as he had sat down on the couch in the front room Anna had led him to. She opened the curtains to let the sunlight fill the room while John took off his jacket. John took a deep breath but felt no relief as if he suffered from asthma from the cold and couldn't catch his breath. Anna leaned into him and placed her hands over his forearms gently coaxing John to give her his hands to hold, but with each breath he rebuked her gentle offering.

Each time Anna's hands went to John and came back empty she tried again reaching out with more ferocity than the last. Anna, sitting beside John trying to reach him, avoided any speech that would sound too much like an adult, but instead she made soothing noises like that of a baby cooing he had no choice but to let her examine his being. With his hands rolled up in hers in a ball, fighting back the tears John spoke softly, "My feelings overwhelmed me. My mind, controlled by emotions, led me back to the past, to the last night I had seen you." He let his eyes fall over Anna's face looking for sympathy.

Anna gave a heartfelt reply as she pulled John's arms close to her breast, "The days you had left home, left your family, left everyone that ever said they loved you including me- I cried just like you are now!" Her tone was turning more reflective and sad as it tuned into John.

His mind began to shoot back and forth in time, from the day he left home to the day he found himself alone walking to the bus, to the present. John pulled back in fear and disgust at Anna's mention of love, but she held onto his hands tightly and looked deep into his face and she suddenly seemed much smaller than John had remembered her. She straightened her posture on the couch and dropped both their hands held together down into the space between their legs. As she spoke John began to memorize her lips and words as he pulled his body to hers, lifting their hands and pressing their legs together. Anna allowed her body to press next to John but pulled her hands away quickly from his like she had freed a dove by sharing her innocent desire with him. Anna stood up and away from John. She reached out her arms inviting him to stand, and as he took her hands and rose from off the couch, she led him by the hand into the kitchen of her house.

As they walked through the hallway into the kitchen John thought he felt relieved after their talk and was pleased to follow her graceful walk. In the kitchen the blue curtains were already open and the sunlight filled the room. Anna led John to the table and gently let go of his hand placing it on his shoulder instead. She smiled warmly down at him and excused herself to the counter where several cut up oranges and a large pitcher of tea lay. John watched her from behind and kept his gaze on her as she moved around the kitchen. He couldn't help but admire her ease and grace as she picked up the slices of fruit and laid them on a large white dish.

Anna could see John watching her and turned keeping his gave as she smiled and brought the fruit to the table, setting it away from her, just away from John. She went back to the counter and carried to the table two clean glasses and the pitcher of tea. Before she sat down she gave John one of the glasses allowing him to slide his glass out from hers, and she sat hers on the table next to his. "John," Anna said softly as she poured tea into his cup. "I want you to know I'm glad you came this morning, I know it wasn't easy because of all the driving." Her eyes concentrated on his face as she spoke her words.

"Yeah, the drive was very interesting, I have kind of wanted to talk to you about some things I was thinking on the way here." said John. Her look was that of intrigue as she listened to him, and she worried that John would be intimidated by her constant glare so Anna turned and filled her own glass looking down at the brown liquid as it poured from the pitcher.

Anna waited for John to speak first perhaps to tell her of his thoughts during the drive to her house, but John was too busy watching her trying to get a read on why she had wanted to see him so badly. John felt it was better not to say too much than to give away his motives for wanting to come, so he asked her, "What other 'stuff' do you think was going to be a problem, besides the driving?" Anna took a sip and pulled the glass away from her lips as she shrugged her shoulders involuntarily. Anna laid her free hand on John's shoulder and stood close enough to him so that he could not look up past her breasts, into her face without straining.

She thought for a moment, aware that John's eyes couldn't reach her, and replied to him, "Other things that may be going on in your life right now. Things we talk about now and again. How is Debbie?" John turned in his chair abruptly as Debbie's name resounded in his ears. He turned so fast that the legs of his chair slid around in a circular motion and he was facing Anna directly.

He could see her face just fine now and said, "We talked about this already, about how we weren't

9

going to discuss Debbie. Any way she's at home, and if that's what's bothering you, you needn't worry."

Anna lost her smile and decided to question him, "John," she said smugly, "Why were you crying outside when you arrived. Don't lie either because you already told me there were things you had on your mind on your way here. And don't be so defensive about Debbie," she managed to smile and say, "You almost made me spill my tea."

John stood up and looked at Anna squarely, but couldn't manage to find any words to say, so he reached toward the glass in her hand and took it into his own as her smile grew and she tried to keep him from doing so. John managed to get the drink from her hand, but reacted too slowly to keep her other arm from flying up and gathering around his neck. Anna couldn't contain her laughter as John took a sip from her cup and slammed it onto the table shaking the table's legs and letting some of the fruit glide off the plate onto its bare surface.

"What are you going to do John," Anna asked as she pulled his large frame closer to her, "if I say things you don't like?" John put both his hands on Anna's waist and raised her off the kitchen tile. Like an experienced dancer she wrapped her legs around his torso and let her body fall into his, her breasts draping down John's neck and her mouth falling across his ear as her warm breath enticed him to continue. John thought then that he could have his way with her easily, but he knew nothing, good could come of it just yet.

He ran his lips over the lobe of her ear and stopped with his mouth just over her silver earing. "Anna, I knew what this was about, why you wanted me here, and I wasn't sure about coming at all." He pressed his mouth against her ear to stall any reaction she might have before he was finished speaking. He squeezed her legs with his hands and Anna released him setting both her feet down onto the tile. "I came because Debbie trusted me enough to come; she told me that if I came it would be good for us."

Anna let her body fall backwards against the wall and looked at John for a moment. "So why didn't Debbie come with you if you two are such good planners. I think all three of us should spend time together if you want to be a part of my life." John looked Anna over carefully as she spoke considering if she was telling the truth or just trying to keep him there longer to seduce him.

To John, Debbie's feelings came first and were all that mattered. It wasn't that he didn't like having Anna for a friend, but it was coming down to Anna asking John to choose one or the other and he chose Debbie. Trust is a forgotten thing to some people. To Anna trust was something that was bright and shimmering and new, something that could be bought or bartered for like a piece of jewelry, but to John trust wasn't so concrete. John always weighed things carefully before proceeding, and now in the moment what seemed like a great opportunity for sex, seemed to John like a bad situation in the making. Feeling remorse for having made a bad situation of things, John wanted to cause as little more damage as possible. Already he had hurt Debbie by coming, hurt Anna by showing up in tears, and soon his opportunity to bang Anna would be the surefire end of all the good in his life leaving him miserable and alone.

"I'm not sure that you and Debbie can cooperate well enough for us to do that Anna." John said as he stepped back from her, "Its best that I go now. I don't want to cause any more pain. I hope you're not mad."

Anna stopped leaning against the wall and crossed her arms as she stood up straight making her seem much taller to John. "I'm still glad you're here John. It's been so long since I've seen you I had almost forgotten how handsome you are. I'm not mad, but not happy either," she shook her finger at John, "I can tell you want to leave and get back to Debbie. I'm not thrilled about your relationship, but that's my own fault. When you get home and things cool down though don't forget me. Give me a call," Anna was inching back to John and caressing his shoulders with her outstretched arms, "if you think we can make this work for the best, ok."

Ch. 2

At home John had slept well past noon, and when he awoke he rolled over in bed pulling the bedspread up around his broad chest, exposing his naked feet. He tried to see through his squinted eyes, but the room around him was a blur. He squeezed his eyes open and shut a few times trying to concentrate his vision on different things around the room.

First, he tried to focus on the large watercolor painting that hung on the wall opposite his bed, but could discern only the vague image of black and white people that seemed to be dancing. Next, he diverted his attention to the small wooden table, but instead of being able to name off the items that sat atop the table, he saw what appeared to be a waterfall. John dozed back off to sleep for what felt to him like eternity, but only turned out to be twenty or so minutes on the clock.

He waited a moment before opening his eyes as if they were stuck fast shut in dread of being opened only to find his eyes exposed but no supply of vision from them. Anticipating the worst, another twenty under the sheets alone, John tried and opened his eyes. This time the feeling of a bright new morning to a great day spread through his bones, and along with the feeling of greatness his 20/20 vision, just as he hoped. The clock next to the bed read eleven fifteen, and John threw the covers off his body dropping his feet to the floor. A chill swept over him as he stood up alone in the room, so he pulled on his thermal shorts over his boxers. In the bathroom adjoining the bedroom John opened the medicine cabinet above the sink.

Without paying much attention to his reflection in the mirror as he swung open the cabinet door there, he reached up and grabbed one of the bottles of pills with his name on it. He opened the bottle and removed a pill, grabbed a paper cup from the dispenser beside the sink and filled it with water, and he downed the pill.

Shawn and John had argued constantly after John's trip to Anna's house, and Shawn had been staying at a house across town with some friends. He still saw Shawn almost every day after he got off work. Shawn would wait in the park downtown for John to arrive and the two of them would stroll through the gardens and exhibits throughout the mile or so long trails.

Shawn would talk about how different it was staying at his friends' house as John listened in earnest. It had seemed to Shawn that John always spoke about his visit to Anna's as they walked. She hadn't requested they both come next time, but Shawn felt John never had any intention of bringing him and thought it was selfishness on John's part. It was on Sunday of the last week of October Shawn had finally given up. He had asked to go to Anna's with John, but John never let anything materialize, no plans, or dates, or anything.

Now, on a cloudy day in November John walked through the park with Shawn as they came upon a vendor's booth. The man at the booth was doing caricatures of the people in the park and had attracted a small crowd of gatherers. As the people stood around and chatted on the work of the artist there were a few good comments and some laughter and an overall murmur around the booth. Shawn and John were both wearing jackets and gloves that matched, black on black. John wore dark brown slacks and Shawn wore his favorite blue jeans. John had a scarf wrapped around his well-built neck, a present from Shawn last winter, and Shawn had a worn cotton pullover with its hood up, under his jacket. John didn't recognize it, but he noticed it was too sun bleached to be new and a bit to out of style.

John asked, "Who does that shirt belong to? Surely, it's not yours?"

Shawn joked, "Its Alan's I think, I'm really not sure I just found it lying around. Why? Do you not like it? Do you think the artist will draw me a funny picture of me in it you can keep?"

John, trying to remain composed, replied, "Joke if you want, but it's cold enough out here to have to wear two of them. How is your friend Alan?" John dropped two dollars onto the counter of the booth as the artist slipped a funny picture of Shawn into his hand. John held up the picture to Shawn as the crowd around them made giggling comments about its being a masterpiece.

John held down the drawing and folded it over in half. Shawn shivering from the cold put his gloved hands in his pockets for a moment as he said to John, "Don't go showing that to anyone." with a hint of sarcasm in his voice.

John questioned Shawn further, "Do you need anything? What about dinner? Will you let me help you Shawn?" Shawn motioned for John to start walking down one of the trails that led through the park and John followed.

As they walked down the path the trees around them grew closer and closer together, choking out the backdrop of city buildings and skyscrapers. A short distance from end of the path it took a long winding turn up a small hill and the trees thinned out just enough to cut out the buildings and noises of the city around them but enough to allow the cloudy sky a chance to drop some sunlight over the ground. The wind picked up and Shawn turned his head over his shoulder to look and see if they were alone, they were. John stood next to Shawn with his back to the wind and asked again, "Do you need anything. I want to help, but you have to let me." Shawn wasn't sure what the right thing to do at this point was.

He had kept away from John's house for a month and felt like things were just getting patched up between them. Shawn wasn't even sure anymore what their fight had been about, and he just wanted it over but didn't know how to tell John. Instead of baring his soul Shawn handed a note to John. John took the note and asked, "What's this, Shawn?

"That, John, is a note from my roommate Alan. Just read it ok, and if you really want to help me then take this address and stop by tomorrow night. I'll be there at six, so try to be there then, and John try to remember please." Shawn grabbed John quickly on both arms and hugged John, pressing his face against his for a last shot of warmth. "Goodbye, John!" Shawn said as he turned and walked off down the path.

"Goodbye, Shawn! I'll see you tomorrow." John replied as he walked down back toward the artist's booth still crowded about with people.

John arrived back home just before dark, pulling his black sports car into the drive and shutting off the ignition. He jumped out of the car and slammed the door shut behind him as he ran up the front steps and unlocked his door. Inside John pulled off his gloves and stuffed them in one jacket pocket and pulling off his hat put it in the other pocket. He hung the jacket on its hanger on the hall wall and went into the kitchen.

He flicked the on the light switch and tossed his keys into a bowl on the kitchen table. He rubbed his hands furiously to warm them and looked up at the ceiling as his eyes began to adjust to the lights. In his pants pocket was the letter, and he took it out laying it on the table in front of him as he sat down.

The chair at the table was an expensive wooden one that he had bought in a set separate from the table. He thought the chairs had looked sophisticated because of the thin wooden armrests each one had. Choosing them over the original set without armrests cost him extra at the furniture outlet, but John had thought the variety well worth the price.

John unfolded the letter placing it squarely in front of him. He held it under the kitchen lights and gave it a quick examination before setting it back down. In the note was just a short few lines in Shawn's handwriting consisting of nothing more than an address to a local bar John was familiar with and the words "John, I love you.", written underneath.

The rest of the note that Shawn had said was from his roommate Alan was about a page long, and it detailed how Shawn had come to live at the house he stayed at, some details about the relationships at the house, and what interested John the most was the last paragraph of the note.

John rested his elbows on the chair and held his hands just off the surface of the table with the note clutched between them as he read the last few lines aloud to himself,

"And after a month of trying Shawn has

finally devised a way of getting Anna back into your life. I told him not to do this but he refused to listen, so I asked him to give you this note making him promise not to read it. I told him it was just a friendly hello since we have never met, but I mean it to be more than that. So if you read this without Shawn knowing what is in it, and you want to know what he is really up to call me at this number. ###-###-#### at five o'clock the day after you receive this note. I want to be as good a friend to Shawn as possible, but I think you should know this." and at the bottom of the letter read, "P.S. - Shawn told me how cool you are!"

John pushed the chair back away from the table just enough so that his outstretched arms hung limply in front of and his hands rested with Alan's letter between them on the edge of the table. The light from the kitchen ceiling poured down over the letter and John cast a naked glance over the heart of it as he deliberated what would be his next move.

He knew from the contents of the letter that Alan had purposefully devised a plan so that if John carried it out he would call Alan just before he was supposed to meet up with Shawn at the bar across town. The only question was why Alan had decided to write this letter and deliver it through Shawn. John had never even met Alan but had been told about him through Shawn. Shawn had told him some time after they had met when John was new to town that he and

19

Alan were once good friends but had stopped talking after high school. John didn't know much more than that about Alan other than the fact that after his fight with Shawn, Alan's had been the first place Shawn went to for help. John leaned closer to the letter in his hands and scrutinized it for any tells that might give away deceit from Alan, but he could find no reason to suspect foul play. He simply had to trust the fact that Alan had information on Shawn that he wanted to share with him.

At work the on the third floor of the high rise office building John carried out his normal routine. In his office he ate lunch getting a salad from the woman who pushed her cart around selling sandwiches instead of going to eat at the deli like he often did on Fridays. He wore his regular cologne that he reserved for days that he wouldn't have time to go home before a meeting and the scent of it carried its usual formidable expression saying to the world that yes he was going past five o' clock, but it didn't bother him. As the end of the day approached John sat behind his desk in the brown leather executive chair he had received with his office.

He stared out the open door to his office and watched as some of the newer employees to the firm walked around frantically trying to get in a few last minutes of work before they left for the day. Recognizing the hour was approaching for him to make his decision, on whether to call Debbie or just show up to meet Shawn, John stood up out from behind his desk and paced the grey room a few times. As he paced he unbuttoned his shirt sleeves and rolled them up over his forearms. The watch on his wrist read four forty five p.m., and John annoyed at his having looked at it grabbed the door and shut it, never missing a pace. He then returned to his desk and took out Alan's letter from the drawer above his knees.

He picked up the receiver to his office phone and set it on the desk face down and watched as the tiny red lights danced away on his desk. He dialed the number in the letter and picked up the phone cradling it between his neck and head as he listened to the pulse waiting for someone to pick up on the other end. John had decided that if Shawn answered he would tell him he did want to meet but at a restaurant around the corner from the originally planned spot.

John thought out the words he would say for every possible response Shawn may have to this just as a voice on the other end of the line spoke, "Alan here."

John shifted the receiver to his other ear and adjusted his posture slightly sitting at attention over his desk. "Alan, good to hear your voice, this is John. Do you know why I'm calling?" spoke John in his business voice.

The voice replied at the other end, "Oh, yes.

Hi. It's nice to finally be able to talk to you. You got my letter then, what did you think?"

John moved slightly back into his chair, "I'm not sure quite what to make of it at the moment, I mean I am supposed to be across town shortly." John had moved back farther into his chair and his voice was giving away his subdued interest in the letter.

"Well John, I think it could be a lot more to your liking if we didn't discuss too much over the phone. Maybe you could just come over, and we can talk about it here." John felt dismantled by the words as Alan spoke each one. He was slumped into his chair and listening to his own breath hiss in his ear from the phone pickup.

John looked at his wristwatch again, four fifty pm. And he was supposed to meet Shawn at Six. John spoke slow and calm into the receiver, "Don't you think that would be a conflict of interest to both parties involved," he joked and let out a choked laugh at his play on words, "Is this going to take long?"

Alan replied, "No John, this is only going to take as long as you want it too, if you want it too." Alan paused listening to John's breath over the line as he continued, "We'll make it as quick as possible though I promise you that, so do you know the address to my place?" John rolled his chair back toward the window and let his arm extend to the drawer as he quietly pulled it open and shut. He was thinking as fast as he could trying to stall for time or come up with an excuse, but all his efforts failed and he accepted the invitation to be at Alan's within the hour.

      John arrived at Allen's condo at quarter past five easing his black sports car in behind the dark red SUV parked in the drive. The house looked nice from the outside painted a dull yellow that looked warm and inviting as John walked through the cold to the entry way. John knocked on the door returning his hands into his pockets to avoid the wind that had blown across the area the last few days. As he waited he hugged at himself under his jacket comforting himself as he looked at the gray sky for any sign of the sun coming back out of hiding.

      Alan opened the door and John saw him for the first time. Alan wasn't as tall as John but he had a build that would put off anyone calling him small. Alan invited him in as John thought Alan must be a weightlifter or a body builder and looked around for any equipment that might prove his suspicions correct. Alan took John's coat and hung it in the hall closet as he asked John to make himself comfortable in the living room. Alan excused himself for a moment and headed off to the kitchen. As John entered the living room he was impressed by the art that hung on its' walls. Several pictures of wildlife scenery looked back at John as he moved around the room examining its contents. Just as John had made his way to the far wall of the room and was handling a small statuette he had found lying on the corner table Alan reappeared from the kitchen and carried with him two beers.

Alan spoke to John, "That is a keepsake I got while on vacation in Miami, Florida. The beaches are beautiful there and the shopping is just as memorable. Do you like it?" John laid the piece back onto the table and moved toward the couch adjacent to the armchair Alan had sat down in upon entering the room.

"It's really nice. I never have been to Florida. Your home though is really nice Allen." Alan sat the beers down in front of him on a glass topped table gesturing for John to have a seat on the couch.

"It is really nice, since I've moved here I haven't had a single complaint." Alan finally let off a wide smile directed at John. "But you didn't come here for no reason at all did you John. You came here for information on Shawn. You want to know what he's up to, and I understand that. Do you drink?" Alan held out one of the beers to John.

John accepted the beer and gave Alan a puzzled smile. "I didn't come here to drink either. And I'm not quite sure what you mean by all this."

Alan stood up from his seat and walked around to the back of it resting his arms over the headrest and cupping his beer in both hands. Again, Alan gave John a wide smile that said he knew more than he was telling and he began, "John we don't know each other very well and although this meeting of ours is a bit at the last minute it's going to be very important to you." John watched Alan from his seat on the couch and tried to relax by sitting back on the soft cushioned material as he drank a cold mouthful of his beer. Alan continued, "I don't want this to be any harder than it has to be, and after I tell you this I'd appreciate it if you took some time to think it over, and didn't just run out that front door. So here goes." As Alan spoke his head moved from side to side and he kept his eyes only half on John and half on his belongings around the room.

"John," said Alan, "Shawn wasn't going to be in that bar tonight to meet you, but you're a smart guy you may have already guessed that much." John adjusted his body on the brown material of the couch in hope that he would be more in line with Alan's sight as if he were about to speak, but he remained silent as he held his beer between his legs with one hand and held his other loosely over his leg pointed in Alan's direction. "So if Shawn wasn't going to meet you, and I can tell you he isn't here. Then its where is Shawn that is the question. You may not believe this so if you need to make a phone call go ahead, as I'm sure you brought your phone and left it in your jacket because in those pants I can't imagine where else you put it."

John was getting to be quite red in the face

now and he could feel the heat rising from and around his neck. "I want you to tell me where Shawn is Alan." he said coldly. "Ok John, Shawn is at your house with Debbie. There I said it, shit, Shawn told me to do this, and he set the whole thing up. You've been too busy to notice that Shawn left last night to go to you and Debbie's. He called her last week and arranged to meet her before she went to work. He explained his situation with you to her since you and he last met, and she agreed. Shawn won't be back until tonight." John looked horrified as he leaned forward placing his beer on the glass of the table in front of him. He looked at Alan still standing behind the chair and gave him a look of despair.

John's hands began to tremble as he sat uprightly on the couch holding his head down and turning it from side to side. He knew Alan was telling the truth about where Shawn was, but he couldn't come to terms with why Shawn would do such a thing. He felt the initial anger subside over thinking Alan was playing games with him as he realized this was all Shawn's doing. He felt his heart give a slight pang of grief and then he became overjoyed at the thought of Shawn being alone with Debbie.

Alan moved from behind the chair and walked toward John from around the glass coffee table, and saw the relief as it entered John's face as he sat next to him on the couch. Alan set down his beer next to John's and put his hand over John's knee

26

rubbing his leg like he was trying to get feeling back into it. John watched as Alan leaned into his body saying reassuring him that Shawn would be fine, and that he would be back in a few hours if John wanted to wait until then with him. John leaned back and rested his head on Alan's shoulder as Allen raised his hand to John's head and stroked his ear softly. Alan's grip tightened on John and John lifted his head to see Alan face to face. Slowly Alan released his grip on John and stared back into his eyes, they were a pale blue set he thought. John could feel Alan's hot breath on his face as a silent code flashed through his eyes forcing Alan to look away. John moved forward on the couch and Alan let go completely saying, "Go ahead, its right around the corner." John gave him a look of intense excitement and hurried off to the hall closet, there he searched through his jacket pockets until he found his cell phone.

Shutting the door to the closet he tried to reacquaint himself with his phone until he realized he felt out of breath. His head was buzzing with excitement and he continued to try to dial Debbie, but the more he tried to focus on dialing the more the buzzing spread throughout out his limbs. His legs started to shake and he managed to the living room where Alan sat back on the couch as if exhausted. John barely made it into the room as his knees buckled and he succumbed to the feeling of drowsiness and fell onto the floor, his cell phone flying out of his hands and sliding across the white carpet a few feet from him.

Alan sprang up from off the couch shouting, "John! What is it? What happened?" Alan fell onto his knees in front of John and slid his hands across John's back to revive him. Just as he tried to turn John's body over to face the ceiling Alan lifted his head to the sound of keys in the front door. As the door opened Debbie stepped through into the hall seeing Alan as he lay over John's lifeless body turned half way up to him with John's lifeless face hanging down toward the floor.

Ch. 3

Elsewhere, Anna lie face down on the bed staring at the television screen in front of her. Her feet raised into the air suspended above the pillows at the head of the bed. Anna's hand hangs over the foot of the bed dragging the remote to the television back and forth across the carpet as if she were drawing a line between her and it. The lamp on the side table beside the bed cast an odd yellow glow no brighter than that of the older modeled digital set in front of her.

On the bed beside her head her cell phone lights up and flashes occasionally with each new text message sent to her from Debbie. They have been texting for the last several hours and each new time

28

the phone's lights flash she looks at it with contempt before picking it up and replying to her. Anna decided ahead of time that at ten o' clock she would take a shower, and her clothes were stacked neatly in the bathroom in front of the mirror.

Ten o' clock came and she eased into the shower turning on the hot water first then gradually turning the knob marked cold. The steam from the water that poured over her filled the room as she washed. She exits the shower and towels off leaving the towel wrapped around her hanging off her breasts. She puts her hair up in front of the mirror and turns away toward the bed, her damp auburn hair trying to fall, loose and bouncing from side to side as she walks. She sits on the bed and checks her phone for any messages she might have missed, but there are none so instead she flings her phone down onto the crisp bedspread as there is a loud knock at the door of the motel room.

When she opens the door to the motel room her eyes met Debbie's. Eyes that were now dry from a long anguished fit, and looking at Debbie, she wondered how it was she had gotten to be in such a state, gone from the bright eyed sojourner into the city to meet John at Alan's.

As she entered the room Debbie began to silently curse, curse manhood, for allowing the world that never loved to try to love her, for allowing herself to love and be loved by men she cursed. Then

Anna brought her to the bed and told her it was ok. Debbie knew kindness was never as common as in the heart of the willing and she shared the story of arriving at Alan's to find John feinted, lying on the floor. Anna listened as Debbie retold the events of the last few hours, "Why did going there lead to so drastic a change from where we had expected it to lead."

Anna had no good answer for her, but she managed to lean beside her slender body and to say, "We tried with pure hearts, like lights in the darkness of the world. We had expectations of gaining ground with John, but when we decide to keep secrets we leave to this place of mad and damned red souls, we forgot what we're doing is dependent on John ."

As Anna spoke Debbie took her phone from out of her jacket, her red watery eyes hung as she recounted the events of the last hour, "So John was passed out and when he snapped out of it and stood his legs felt loose beneath him, so he had to pause to lean against the table with one hand on Alan's shoulder. As he stood inanimate waiting to be dragged away toward the couch Alan got upset and started to shout at me like everything was my fault. Before I knew it Alan was helping John to the couch, demanding that I leave." Debbie's speech was full of life at, and at her side with her heart racing Anna prayed for a new beginning, or a land of promise never dreamed of by the heart.

Anna spoke, "Then what we need is a place to finally get John without our being meshed in with others opinions, others that can't tell us were wrong- like Alan." Debbie got up from off the bed and raced through the bathroom door, and a moment later reappeared with a toothbrush fumbling in her hands. She felt the cold creep into the inner mesh of her open jacket and stopped a minute to listen as Anna made proposal after proposal for ways they might still win over John.

Anna sat on the bed's edge, her hair now dry and the towel around her breasts beginning to sag loosely just over her nipples, with the light from the muted screen of the television dancing on the reflective surface of the bed's nylon fabric. As Debbie stood in the bathroom she took off her jacket and curled it up into a ball throwing on the floor of the motel room. "Anna," she said as she rinsed the toothbrush, "this is not working. You said that John would be here already but he's still back at Alan's place. Alan told him Shawn was at my house, not here in this motel, and John didn't see me before I left Alan's. Now you had better have a plan because it was you who seduced me into following you here to this Motel."

Anna stared at Debbie from the bed, "I seduced you into coming here? You had sex with me, remember. You were the one, who just had to have John back so bad, so why would you be mad at me?"

31

Debbie returned to the floating lights around the bed and stood over Anna. Her head swirled as she stared down at her, all the colors of the room moving around like a large carousel. She stood a moment until she understood what Anna had meant, until she felt the anger toward her, and she calmed herself with deep heavy breaths.

"Anna, I'm not mad at you. I'm mad at John. Thinking I could trap him here in this Motel room with you was a mistake I'm sorry I made." Debbie said as she sat back on the bed.

Anna looked relieved and asked Debbie, "John doesn't know I'm here with you does he?" Debbie answered with a head nod. "Good. We just won't tell him. When John wakes up at Alan's he won't know we were going to bring him here and seduce him. But we shouldn't go back to Alan's tonight, not while he's still mad." Debbie watched as Anna let the towel around her fall onto the bed and noticed how erect her nipples had become.

Debbie pulled up her shirt to remove it, but already Anna's hands were caressing her chest. "Promise me." Debbie said as the two lay back on the stiff bed.

Already Anna was on top of her, hair falling around her shoulders, "We shouldn't have come here Debbie."

Debbie awoke at five a.m. and sat up in the

bed with her back pressed against the headboards. She cried a while and as the tears receded she knew there were no imaginary pictures which haunted over her mind's inner recesses. Debbie knew that she had done the unthinkable and Anna's very real body lie under the covers with her, not just an encountered ghost in the night. The first specks of daylight shown through the window and reminded her of home, but she didn't know just how far away from home she had gotten .

Ch. 4

The next morning Alan was standing in the kitchen of his condo making jam and toast along with his routine coffee when he heard the doorbell ring. He left his breakfast on the counter and turned down the hall towards the door momentarily noticing the spot John had fallen the night before. Alan looked back over his shoulder toward the bedroom where John was sleeping and he wondered if perhaps it was Shawn, that maybe he had lost his keys. Alan opened the door pulling the handle slowly, but he didn't recognize the beautiful women standing outside. She was tall and had long auburn hair just as Shawn had described Anna to him, so he asked, "You must be Anna, right. I'm Alan. Where is Shawn?" The sun shone over the shoulders of his unannounced visitor blacking out her face.

"I don't know where Shawn is, but Debbie is getting her things out of my car. She'll be just a minute. Is John still here, Alan?" the woman said.

"So you're Anna. John is still recovering from his spell last night, and I think its best not to disturb him." Alan said trying to look out the door past Anna.

"High Alan is John all right. I was so scared last night after leaving so I checked my phone every fifteen minutes for a message. He's still here isn't he?" Debbie had appeared from behind Anna with her overnight bag as she spoke.

Alan replied, "Yeah he's here, but I just told Anna were going to let him get out of bed when he's ready." Anna nodded approvingly. Debbie carried her bag into the hall walking past Alan and inviting Anna to make herself comfortable in the living room. She almost accepted before Alan said to both of them, "I've got some coffee going in the kitchen."

Alan, as he closed the door, gave Anna a quick once over and then headed for the kitchen. Anna noticed for the first time how muscular Alan was as he walked past her indifferently. She was much taller than he yet she imagined him as formidable as she followed him into the kitchen. Alan gave Anna a seat at the table and poured her coffee into a white mug. He went to the counter and returned to the table with a cup of milk and a bowl of sugar placing them in front of Anna.

Debbie came into the doorway to the kitchen

behind Anna and watched Alan closely as stood. Alan gave Debbie a smile and poured her a cup at the table. As they all took their seats at the table a silence filled the kitchen outside of the clinking of cups on saucers and the little sipping noises made by the three as they drank. Anna spoke first, "I feel odd being in your home in such strange circumstance Alan. It really is a beautiful place you have here. How long have you lived here?"

Alan smiled and replied, "I few years. Shawn and I went to high school together. We were quite close at one time. I've just been helping him out lately with a place to stay. How long have you and John been arguing?"

Anna was surprised by Alan's forthrightness, but answered, "Not long really. We just met the other day, and Shawn called me about the time he came to stay here to live with you."

Alan was pleased and asked Debbie, "I wondered how much of the truth you have been telling Shawn. After last night I assumed you were lying about things to get to John. So please, tell me how you met Anna."

Debbie was not pleased by Alan's question, but felt she must answer to clear up any misgivings, "Ok Alan, if you want to play games. I found her number in John's belongings while John was visiting her last month. I was worried things would go badly between them, and I found myself in his personal room. I saw a photograph of her with her number on the back and I took it." Debbie was speaking softly as if the memory was unbearable enough already, "Later, after John refused to introduce me to Anna," Debbie said this as she motioned with her coffee cup in Anna's direction, "I decided I would introduce myself. You know the rest already Alan because you and Shawn have been my help in this entire affair since then."

"Not so fast," Alan spoke, "There are things I know, and there are things kept secret. But there are some things you aren't aware of yet as well. Last night while you were who knows where Shawn came in late. He had a layover on his business flight for a few hours and came in an hour or so after you left."

Debbie was confused and asked, "What does that have to do with anything Alan?"

"Where should we start? How about with Anna, so Anna how did you meet Shawn?" Alan crossed his arms as if he had accomplished a victory with his question, and he waited for an answer.

"Alan, Anna doesn't know Shawn. She has never been here before. What are you talking about?" Debbie answered angrily. Alan looked straight ahead in innocence, "Shawn saw John sleeping in the bedroom and he recognized him. I asked him if he was sure and he said, yes. So I showed him the bottle of pills he'd dropped as I carried him into the spare room and he recognized them too."

Anna thought for a moment and asked Alan for a picture of Shawn. Alan went off to the bedroom and returned with a portrait of Shawn from high school and handed it to Anna. She stared at the picture a moment then set it down flat on the table. She returned to drinking her coffee as she spoke, "This is Shawn Thawing. Shawn introduced me to John four years ago."

Grateful, but startled, Alan never asked what she and Debbie had done last night, Anna told the story of their encounter with Shawn, "We all met at a club. I don't really remember meeting, but four years ago he was there with John. I do remember it as the first time I was introduced to John though."

"She'll tell you all about it if you like." spoke John from the hall outside the kitchen. The three faces at the table all turned in the direction of John's voice. There in the opening between the hall to the bedroom and the kitchen stood John. He had been listening to them talk since they'd sat down. John wore the pants he had on the night before and no shirt. He walked to the kitchen counter and poured a glass of coffee as he told them the story of the first time he was introduced to Debbie, "The man you're talking about introduced himself to me as Mr. Thawing. And yes he was married, to a Native American girl from the reservation. I questioned him once on the difference between the two of them, and he politely explained that she was from a reservation in northern New York, and he was a shade paler of European descent. He was the manager of a motel on the edge of the city here at which I stayed when I first moved to this city. Thawing was turning out to be quite nice and made all the arrangements for my stay in one of the upper rooms of the motel."

"Well, one night several weeks into my stay I had ventured out alone, without Thawing at my side, and came upon a local club I was somewhat familiar with. There seemed to be a large congregation forming outside as if the owner of the establishment had closed for the night and shut out all the patrons in the night air, which was becoming more cold as the weeks had passed. As I strayed through the lines and circles of people there I saw Mr. Thawing, Shawn, standing with a woman at his side, and not his wife either. I watched the two, examining Thawing's grey coat, and the girl next to him was strikingly different than his wife. The girl was much taller than Thawing's wife and skinnier too. She wore a blue overcoat and had beautiful long hair, and her face was offset by the rosiest red color of lips. Thawing saw me as I watched the two of them, and they approached me in a fashion, a bit too speedy, a bit too merry.

We engaged ourselves in conversation in the night air, and I began to realize that my conversation bored the girl. Thawing wasn't the least shy in his interests toward the girl as he's standing in front of me, why should he have been I suppose; I was no threat to him. I was uncomfortable and excused myself as soon as I had a chance. "John Handy, you have to learn to live more!" came out of him later back at the motel. He told me the sweet innocent girl at the club had wanted me to stay, and that I should have because he had ended up going back to her place."

All three at the table stared at John in disbelief. Anna spoke outright angrily to John, "His name is Shawn, so you don't have to keep calling him by his last name."

Alan defended himself to John, "I know that managing a chain of motels is hard work, and that Shawn travels so he's not here that often but what you're saying is in the past. Shawn and his wife are separated."

Debbie puzzled by the story set down the bottle of pills and questioned John, "I thought you had met Anna beside a lake."

John realized his story had confused some, and angered some, of his friends at the table and said, "Well, yeah Shawn, and his wife were very unhappy and this happened years ago. And I only said Anna and I ended our relationship years ago by the lake, and that's true. The initials are still in the trunk of the tree, and the lake is in the city park."

Alan sensing the tension in the room said, "That's it then, we'll all four of us go to the lake this afternoon. I know a guy who sells flowers in the park, and under the counter he sells marijuana. We can go there and smoke out beside the lake and check to see if the initials are there."

John looked pleased with the idea and said, "Ok Alan, I'm feeling better already. I'm in."

Anna and Debbie just shook their heads in agreement to the plan as they donned their jackets, hats, and gloves. After John had picked up the bottle of pills explaining they were only heart medication Alan led John to his clothes in the bedroom. Alan left him to shower to dress himself in private.

In no time, John exited the bedroom and entered the kitchen as his friends were already coming in and out the front door with bags of clothes, blankets, and food for a picnic at the park. Once they had loaded everything into Alan's SUV and situated themselves they closed the doors and Alan turned the key sending the SUV's motor to life.

Ch. 5

At the entrance to the park nearest the lake the four of them all got out of Alan's black SUV. Stepping down and out they each were dressed in their warmest of winter clothes. Anna wore a long dark brown leather overcoat that trailed down to her knees, a blue scarf, and a brimmed brown hat pulled down to her ears. Debbie wore a black leather jacket as did Alan and John, but she did so only under protest from John that she borrow one from Alan. All of them wore gloves, the men's were black and Anna and Debbie's were white.

They all followed Alan up the path to his friend's flower booth. Alan approached his friend at the booth as the rest of the group stood a few feet from it admiring the flowers on display questioning how they were kept alive in such cold weather. Alan's friend was a dark skinned looking Indian and he laughed as he saw Alan reaching out to shake his hand. The two talked at the flower booth for a moment and the dark skinned man reached under the counter out of sight. His hand came up from under the booth's counter and met Alan's with a quick handshake as booth of the men smiled exchanging goodbyes. Alan walked away from the booth to his friends and gestured that they continue walking to the lake just up the path at the clearing.

As they arrived at the edge of the lake from the clearing Anna looked around while she held her hat with one hand simultaneously shielding the sun from her eyes. John motioned for the three others to follow him to the place where the tree once stood. Debbie asked, "Where are we going? This is all still part of the clearing." John kept walking as the others stopped to discuss the location they were after.

Alan asked, "Are we in the right place Anna.

Do you remember where it was?"

"It was right here. But I don't see it now. It's been years since I was here last." replied Anna. "It's right here, so come on." yelled John. They all walked along the edge of the lake towards John. The lake was beautiful and shining as they strolled past, and its waters were still and blue under the sunlight.

They reached John at the far eastern edge of the lake, a distance from where they had emerged from the path, and stood next to him. Before John was the stump of a tree three feet in diameter cut down during the last renovation by the city of the lake front by the city. "It was right here, but it's been cut down now. I'm sure this was it, we can still use the stump to sit around and smoke weed though."

They all agreed that John's plan was fitting, and they sat around the tree stump on all sides. "They'll probably be back in the spring to remove the last of the tree." Alan said as he poured out the contents of the small bag he had got at the flower booth.

"I can't believe it's not here. Where's the proof of all those years. We missed out this time." said Debbie as she helped Alan to break up the weed and pull out the seeds.

Anna fumbled in her purse as she looked down and said, "Can't prove it, but it was here. This was the tree that John had told you guys about. I'm sure of it." looking up at John and handing him a pack of rolling papers she carried in her purse she said, "I'm sorry, John."

"It's ok, the memories are still here." John took out a rolling paper and took the small pile that Alan and Anna had made on top of the stump, a pinch of bright green pot. "At least I still have the dollar you gave me with the same inscriptions as the tree had", spoke John. Anna smiled a deep gay smile and leaned into John. She reached her hand under his jacket into his pants pocket and pulled at his wallet.

John smiled back at her as she lifted his wallet and he moaned in ecstasy as she pulled out the folded dollar bill from within it. "I remember this." she said as she unfolded the dollar bill and John carefully handed her the rolling paper with just the right amount of pot sitting in its crease. Anna took the paper from John carefully and used the dollar bill trick to roll a perfectly shaped joint. She held up the joint when she was done and stretched out the dollar bill on the tree stump face up. Anna handed the joint to John and his lighter was ready in his hand as he took it.

John lit the joint and inhaled deeply as it burned, and with one hand on the dollar and the joint in the other hand he passed it to Debbie on his left. She took a drag and passed it to Alan whom then in turn took a big puff from off it while he used his free hand to remove the joint from his mouth and pass it in Anna's direction. And around and around it went

43

each person performing the same ritual of a deep relaxing toke and a pass of the joint until they were all smiling at one another with inward joy.

The joint continued to spin in John's head as he finished it, and the stump of the tree began to turn green as the dollar he had kept his hand pressed down upon, to stop the wind from stealing it from Anna's view, stretched itself out encompassing its remains. The shape of the heart and the initials inside it began to change and became the shape of a map.

No ordinary map, the tree stump began to glow bright green, and as the shapes and numbers slowly traveled in circles over the dollar as it grew and swelled into a globular shape, as tall as the remains of the tree were wide, slowly the lines connected as if they reached inside the globe and began to materialize. The shapes moved and turned within the globe as John sat mesmerized waiting for some sense to come out of it.

First, the recognizable image of John appeared within the globe. He was speaking to a doctor about his heart condition. The doctor was telling John that he needed relaxation and as the Doctor reached into his pocket extracting a folded dollar bill the image vaporized. Next, an image appeared of Shawn and Anna sitting in a bar formed within the globe. The two sat in a comfortable looking booth and Shawn had the folded dollar bill in his hand outstretched to Anna telling her something

John couldn't quite make out, but this image turned to dust within the globe. Finally, an image of Alan as a young man appeared. The image was of Alan and Shawn standing at a bus stop. The image of Shawn's figure turned away and walked into a boutique as the one of Alan was left standing at the bus stop. As the bus pulled up John debarked it, and Alan approached him and began giving him directions to a motel nearby. And then the image disappeared, and the globe burst into thousands of tiny red embers all floating into the sky.

"Now what's going on?" John asked as he woke from his daydream, and joined with his friends at the corner of the park lake. They were all still high from the marijuana, and they sat close together staring out over the lake to forget their troubles.

"I want to see Shawn again. I want to see if he remembers me." blurted out Anna.
Debbie spoke as he sat next to her, with no one on the other side, "But Alan could tell you that Anna. He saw Shawn last night." Debbie bent forward and looked at Alan sitting on the other end of the line of friends.

"I could tell you, or I could just let Shawn tell you for himself." Alan stood up braving the cold and coddling himself between his arms, his thick black coat and hat disguising him from the onlookers in the park.

"Alan, Shawn is out of town on business.

How is he going to tell Anna anything?" Debbie said with a look of suspicion.

Alan, looking away from Debbie and the group, turning to gaze out over the lake into the sunset over the cities numerous structures replied, "It's easy. Shawn is staying at the Red River Inn. He's training new managers for a couple of weeks and we could drive there in an hour or two. Shawn would give us a room. He has the power to do that, to give us one of the nicest rooms in the place." Alan turned back toward his friends searching their faces for a response.

Anna smiled at him and pushed herself off the ground with both hands, coming up and throwing her arms around Alan's neck. She yelled into his ear, "It's a great idea. We have the whole weekend to get away, and my bags are already packed. You guys have money right? We can go shopping for what we don't have with us while there's still daylight." Anna stood beside Alan holding his hand that had dropped to his side as she had grabbed him to hug. "Well, John, Debbie, what do you two say. Can we go?" She knelt with her gloved hand still holding onto Alan's as she waited for an answer.

Anna gave her best smile and stared down John and Debbie as they sat apart from one another. Debbie stood and looking at John said, "I'm in. I'd like a quick get away, and I'm feeling up to it. John, what about you? You haven't been feeling too well

46

lately and you've had a rough night last night. Your heart condition is worrying me lately."

"Well, if all you're going to do is worry. I called the doctor this morning before I got up. He said I missed my last three doses of medication, and not to let that happen again, so I took my pill and I have more with me in case there's a problem."

Debbie looked John square in the face, "So you can go?"

"Yeah," John stood up throwing his arms into the air in a gesture of release and excitement, "I'm in. Let's go to see Shawn. I'd like to see him myself, after all."

"Great, I get to drive!" Alan mentioned as the four of them huddled near each other discussing the details of the trip.

"Drive if you want to Alan, but we're going shopping first thing!" Anna said deftly with her finger pointed in Alan's face.

Ch. 6

Four hours later, at the Red River Inn, Anna and Alan stood at the reception desk inquiring for the third time why they couldn't see Shawn. The girl behind the desk, wearing a name tag identifying her only as Rita, grew frustrated and asked them politely to sit down and wait for Shawn to come back from his meeting with the Hotel executives. The two of them reluctantly sat in the waiting area with their coats and jackets in their laps and their gloves and hats in their hands. They were chatting with a married couple. The couple was an older guy with no hair and a round stomach wearing a suit, and his wife which was an overweight woman with blond hair wearing a full sized blue dress. Each time the round little man spoke his wife would kick back and let out a loud annoying laugh meant for everyone nearby to hear.

Shawn walked off of the elevator and into the waiting room to see Anna and Alan sitting and chatting with the older couple. He walked up and sat next to Alan whom was sitting farthest away from the talkative old man and his wife. Shawn folded his jacket over his lap and looked flustered. "They said it's his heart. He can't leave now, and he's going to need a lot of sleep before he does." Shawn reported, "And you two will have to stay in a separate room."

Alan nodded approvingly, but Anna asked, "Why can't we see John?" Alan nodded in agreement, "Because Debbie asked us not to just yet, ok Anna."

The hotel bed squeaked as John tossed over onto his side in his sleep. Debbie sat inside the room scribbling on a note card and noticed every move as he slept. She was like a nurse recording his vital signs on a clipboard. Debbie finished writing on the card and exited the room pulling the heavy wooden door shut behind her and turning off the lights.

After she had gone, and the only light

remaining in the room was the small bedside lamp on the desk that was left on, John rolled over onto his back again and continued dreaming as his parched lips moved without sound and sweat dripped from his forehead.

In his dream John had gone back to his motel room after meeting Shawn Thawing and Anna, and he had pulled his suitcase out from under the motel bed slamming it down over the purple bedspread, the suitcase opening from the shock of his hurry. He moved over to the night stand and opened all the drawers and began ripping his clothes out of one drawer after the other, tossing and throwing his belonging in the general direction of the open suitcase, more often than not hitting around it, but mostly his things just landing on the bed or on the floor. He moved over to the bed after the drawers were empty in the night stand and grabbed handful after handful of shirts and jeans, socks, and underwear shoving them all into the suitcase. At last when he was finished he jerked the lid of the suitcase down and closed the lock on each side. Pulling the suitcase down onto the floor next to him as he collapsed, John leaned back against the bed and cried until he fell asleep.

Shawn entered the room as John slept. Like a doctor wearing a long white gown reserved for only the resident staff of a Hospital Shawn moved to the desk into the light with Debbie following behind him. Now in his long white coat the doctor stood and read the name on the patient's chart aloud as he stood beside the machine, "John Handy." Slowly, as the Doctor stood at the bedside Debbie sat in the chair to the left of the bed, and John noticed the Doctor was Shawn.

John came to and opened his eyes looking the man in the white coat directly in the face. Shawn held the card Debbie had prepared in both hands before John in his bed and smiled. He looked over the card and then at John's face and spoke quietly, "How long has it been my friend? Your friend Debbie is here to see you." he smiled, "It'll be a week before you can leave this bed again on your own John."

The doctor patted John's shoulder with one hand, and went to the foot of the bed replacing the chart where it belonged. He then walked to the door and nodded to the Nurse as to give consent for her to stay in the room with John. Debbie could only think to herself in the silence that followed alone in the room that she had met the doctor before, many years ago.

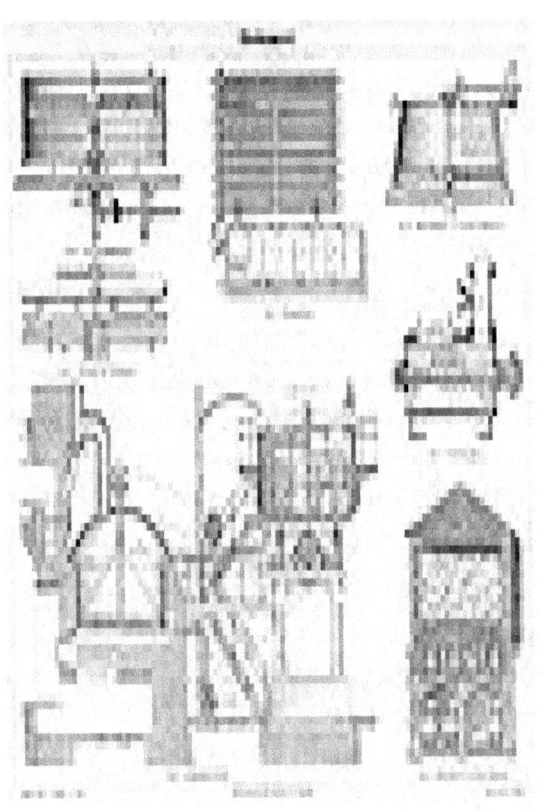

Part II

Ch. 7

"Calm down. Nothing is going to hurt you. You're out of line. Please stop crying! I wanted to see you leave so badly that night just to make you happy, but my heart had no control of my senses and my mind created its own pictures, images, and feelings and all of them of you and her together, and from my guilty senses and never wanting to let you go, I lost control."   John awoke in the hospital bed alone. He opened his eyes and the light of the room sent his senses reeling. He closed his eyes for a moment and watched the red and black shadows as they moved throughout his mind. He attempted again to open his eyes this time in spilt second intervals of open and closed to try to adjust to the light. His eyes moved nervously and shot images of the room that quickly mixed in to the memories of the dreams still within John's head.

As he tried to focus in on single objects to allow some clarity to his sight he chose various objects throughout the room. The large black screen of the television floating in one corner of the room, the brown wooden door with the large silver handle that opened out into the room's toilet, and beside him the IV machine that towered over the corner of the

52

bed like a science fiction coatrack trying to hand him a drink of some clear fluid. John recognized where he was now that he was in this hospital room, and he remembered the rules about patients getting out of bed without calling the nurse station first.

John ignored the rule as he always did on these routine visits of his to rooms just like these, and he began by tossing his stiff numbed legs over the side of the white lined bed. He rose up off the bed and as his legs began to give out underneath him as they did routinely he grabbed at the tall iron bars of the contraption that once stood over him feeding his body the clear fluids from the IV bags. Luckily for John it had wheels and he struggled to move them booth into the bathroom behind the large brown door.

Inside the hospital bathroom John stood in front of the large mirror over the sink. He squinted from the bright incandescent lights that turned on by sensing the patient's movement. He looked ghastly and pale, and one arm had blood running down it. He watched as the blood dripped onto the cold tile floor beside his bare feet, and he realized he was alone in the room for the first time.

The wires and tubes that had followed him from his bed were now creating a silver blue puddle on the floor outside the door, a puddle that was creeping under the door and meshing with the drops of John blood. He turned on the sink by tapping the round handle with the ball of his fist and moved his hands together under the warm flowing water. There was a rack with a single wash cloth and a towel between the sink and the shower that stood next to it, and John picked up the washcloth and held it under the water from the sink. He slowly moved the washcloth up and down his bleeding right arm as he examined closely the tear marks the IV's needle had made as it was torn out from under his skin.

John was never one to doubt the validity of the things that he saw. He was one who believed in what was seen like the old expression, but what frightened John were often the things that he didn't see like the moment between the needle tearing out of his arm and the blood hitting the floor. Done with washing the blood from his arm he grabbed at the toilet paper dispenser and took a small piece of the paper and wedged it between his upper and lower arm at the front of his elbow to stop any further bleeding. He opened the door again and pushed at it from the silver handle, but something was obstructing the door from fully opening. He figured it was the IV and tried to slip through the crack he had made hoping it would be large enough, and he managed to escape back into the room with his bed. Instead of going back to the bed however he decided it was a bad idea and he would have to explain himself to the nurse, so he went instead to the door that led out of the room into the hospital corridor where he could stroll free down the halls. Outside his room a few faces of the other patients, some accompanied by their nurse, turned in his direction, and he noticed that they wore the same square checkered blue, grey gowns as he did.

John was a well-built man with a muscular frame, not that of a competition bodybuilder but enough so that he wasn't intimidated by others easily. He was not as tall as some of his friends either, but he wasn't looked down on by other being between five and six foot. His hair was usually let loose and long, down to his neck, in a honey brown color, but he had a darker beard that had grown-in the last few days he had been staying at the hospital because of his heart condition.

John was hardly noticed as he moved down the corridor of the hospitals east wing where he was being kept under observation. At the nurses' station he kept left of the central area which was a round cubicle with nurses moving in and out from behind its grey carpet covering as they answered phones and lifted clipboards. John kept to the wall at the left of the station and moved along it towards the recreation area that patients were allowed to use on request. He managed to stay unnoticed by anyone and sat in the far seat of the recreation area from the nurses.

There in his seat he was allowed to look out of the glass doors, but no one was permitted to go outside unaccompanied without a nurse, and the door was locked with the only keys being any one of the nurses' badges. But there was a phone that let the patients dial out situated just beside the door which was now just above John's head as he sat in the lounge chair. He moved back as far as he could into the red and brown fabric of the cushioned chair and slowly eased the feet of the chair back and around until he had it right up against the corner of the wall that jutted out and away from the station. Here he was completely out of sight of any nurses who were not busy, and John knew the chance of a nurse coming up to him and asking questions was greater if they were not doing anything.

The phone was built in place so that the patients would have privacy as they used it. It was allowed to dial outside numbers as long as they were local, and a patient didn't have to have permission to use it. The only trouble was that it was so high up on the wall anyone that wished to use it had to be standing.

John was worried that a passing nurse or doctor would recognize him if they happened to be doing their rounds and entered his room. He knew they would be looking for him soon, so he hoped to dial out quick and arrange for a ride to meet him at the ambulance doors. John reached up to grab the phone, but he couldn't quite manage to remove it from off its base so he used his legs to push himself up into the back of the chair supported by the wall. A few inches off of the seat he took down the phone's cold black handle and rested between his neck and shoulder as he turned a little to get a good look at the number he was dialing on its base.

After finally getting the numbers pushed in he relaxed and slumped back into his seat noticing the scenery through the glass doors of snow, wind, and sleet. The phone continued to ring inside the headset as John watched the colored lights of the holidays flicker and flash beyond the great glass doors of the hospital.

"Hello."

"Yeah, hello. I need to be picked up as soon as possible."

"Where are you?"

"I'm at County Hospital in Eldridge."

"Where you headed?"

"Not far from here, but hurry up. I mean A.S.A.P."

"Alright we got a cab coming your way. Should arrive in the next ten minutes. I need your name and the door to pick you up at for the driver."

"My name is John Handy, and listen the driver needs to pick me up in the back at the ambulance entrance. I'll be standing outside, ok."

"Ok, cash or credit?"

John stretched his arm up and put the handset back on its base as quickly and quietly as possible as he himself stood up from out of the chair that had felt so comfortable and now was such a shame to leave. Another different kind of shame was on John's mind though as he walked back along the wall past the nurses' station toward his room. What was he going to do if he got caught now?

John was going back to his room to get his clothes, but with the mess he had in the room he knew the hospital staff would be looking for him very soon. So he did what he had to do, John walked past the first nurse in the long bright-lit corridor, and he innocently bumped into her as she moved past him. The nurse was a tall blond female with a large chest and brown eyes wearing the standard nurse's white uniform that made John question every time he saw one what the hell was a candy striper anyway. The woman looked john over as he passed apologetically moving down the hall, and she stopped just a moment to notice that John had blood on his patient's gown. She began to walk away toward another hall, but stopped and turned going instead to the nurses' station and leaning over the grey circle of desks and speaking to someone behind it. John paused after passing the nurse and leaned against the hall's wall turning his head to see the woman as she leaned into the station.

John admired her form and turned his head back to looking straight down the hall. Just a foot in front of John's body as he leaned on the wall was a red square with a white handle that he took hold of and pulled down hard on the white handle with his right arm. As the wad of toilet paper fell from off of

58

John's arm as he extended John watched it fall. Before it even hit the ground red lights overhead began to circle and flash just as a downpour of water from the ceiling's sprinklers washed over the people in the hall.

The corridor was at least a hundred, maybe two hundred, feet in length and now at regular intervals of five to fifteen feet either a red light secured to the ceiling under a globe rhythmically flashed or a three inch metal prong attached to the hospital's sprinkler system spun wildly shooting out millions of drops of water. John's feet slipped in the water as it filled the hallway and he moved like an ice skater down the hall sliding his feet against the tile and bracing his body against the wall until he reached the door to his room.

As he entered the room he heard the sounds of the staff and patients' yells fill the hall, and he tried not to turn and look but hurried to the dresser on which sat a large plastic bag containing his civilian clothes.

John lifted the bag up with its opening facing down and dumped his clothes out onto the dresser. He discarded the now soaked hospital gown and slipped on his blue jeans sans underwear. He put on the red cotton pullover with the hood that he had worn into the hospital and picking up the dirty socks he had worn decided to throw them on the floor of the room with his wet gown. He pulled on a brown pair of shoes and laced them quickly not bother to double knot them, and not caring if they stayed laced. Last, he discarded the plastic bag itself on to the floor and he held up his black leather jacket, it was still in perfect shape, as he turned toward the door and exited the room. Outside in the hall it was pandemonium with nurses and doctors trying to escort patients off the hall into the larger front lobby of the hospital.

With his jacket tossed over his head and his body still braced up against the wall John moved against the tide of people as they hurried to get to the lobby. He moved in the opposite direction toward the ambulance doors at the rear of the hospital. John watched as he slipped past the now abandoned nurses' station as the woman he had bumped into was still leaned over the desk but was now shouting into a telephone for help. Past the station John got to the ambulance doors without a hitch and pressing against the large steel bar that granted access in and out of the painted red and white doors he was free.

Outside the large double doors of the ambulance ramp conditions weren't much better. The snow and sleet John had seen from the glass doors of the rec area had grown worse and there were people outside in a panic as to what was happening inside. John pulled into his jacket and looked out through the wind and snow for the familiar yellow cab. At the far end of the small parking lot was the cab with the motor running and the window wipers pushing around specks of snow.

John walked a few feet out past the doors and latched on to the metal railing that surrounded the elevated platform he stood on and made his way to the icy stairs. He descended the steps with care and ran, without looking back, to the car as it sat waiting. As he approached the driver leaned over to the passenger side and opened the door a few inches, so John gratefully opened the door, jumped into the cab shutting the door behind him, and gave the driver a huge smile of thanks and appreciation.

Ch. 8

New Year's Eve in the heart of the 5th largest city in the USA can be a very loud place. One side of the city is filled with the noises of the industrial plants and manufacturing houses. On the other side of the city the stillness of night is interrupted each morning with the sounds of commuter traffic and the daily crews of men arriving to continue building construction throughout the blooming residential areas. Nowhere is there absolute peace and quiet, but on the other hand at the heart of the 5th largest city in the USA can be found a place that never sleeps soundly. The downtown area of the city is at a constant high level of excitement especially on an event such as the New Year's.

Deep in the heart of the city is a hotel. Its

name is the Red River Inn, and it is stationed in good proximity to the city's river, thus the Red River. The hotel was built in the 1800's, but it has constantly been renovated throughout the decades of its existence. It is a fourteen story hotel, with no thirteenth story, and it is a somber color of old fashioned red brick and mortar. It stands majestically alongside the Red River with its golden entrance, golden curtains, and golden name written high above the city towering in twenty foot letters on its rooftop.

The residents of the city, either the suburban commuters from the city's surrounding residential districts or the downtown locals residing in its high rise apartment complexes, know the hotel as a landmark that has been with the city as far back as any can remember. Many of the older residents in the city, many of whom live closest to the outskirts of the city, people who still know their neighbors and their families for generations back, those that though have not visited the motel since its latest renovation a few years back, these types of people still remember the stories of their parents staying at the hotel on anniversaries and honeymoons. Other residents of the city, those whom have come to the city in recent years to create homes and families, the people that drive newer cars and keep their children in private schools, the suburbanites and the dwellers of the farthest outreaches of the city, these are those that know the motel as the old historic point of their commute to their new high paying job, and also as their occasional weekend getaway when they want to get away.

      After the hotel was last renovated a few years ago the ownership and management was changed around by the shareholders of the old hotel. Consultants and professionals were brought in to make sure the money spent on the hotel was not given over to waste. Decorator's fees and union contractor's fees for the bricklayers and carpenters caused uneasiness in the shareholders pockets, so new people were sent in to replace older employees. A great stir was made in the atmosphere of the downtown district and stories and rumors were amassing among locals, few of them were true.

      A new manager was brought in the years of renovation, and he has stayed with the hotel to this day. He was once the manager of a chain of several smaller hotels throughout the state, and has always been a favorite among the patrons that have visited his hotels. His name is Shawn Thawing, age 28. He is tall and thin, but still well built more like a basketball player than a football player. He has dark curly hair that is kept short to maintain a professional look, and he always wears business attire most often in gray slacks and jacket, a pressed white shirt, and dark brown dress shoes polished to the point that they resemble the hardwood floor of the hotel.

      New Year's Eve at the Red River is always an

exciting time. People from all over the state and surrounding area come to stay at the hotel for its location and its atmosphere. Parties on the streets downtown outside the motel are not at all uncommon, and party goers often hang outside the bars and taverns as the night draws on and the festivities pick up. The hotel itself hosts such festivities in its spacious and luxurious restaurant and bar the Red Oyster. Well off couples can enjoy drinks and dinner at one of the many tables in the restaurant or they can just drink in the bar lounge and converse with other couples staying for the weekend. The real draw for the crowds of hotel visitors, and any other guests that just come in for the party at the Red Oyster, is the dance floor. The reserved side of the Oyster is cleared of all tables and is highly decorated the night before New Year's Eve, and Hotel Manager Shawn Thawing is in complete control over his staff as they prepare for the bash.

Shawn and his crew of ten staff members specifically assigned to preparing the Oyster are busy from ten o'clock the day before until eight o'clock on the day of the bash preparing. They arrange the tables and dance floor. They hang green and yellow banners, they fill the hall with balloons, and they ready the lights and music. Shawn himself is involved in a frenzy of activities the hours before the party begins, and he still finds time to do his routine duties at the hotel such as taking care of guest's needs and calling staff meetings to address certain members of the staff. The hotel itself has just over two hundred rooms that are available daily for occupancy to guests, and the required number of staff for day to day operations is around forty including the management. Shawn is the head manager of the hotel since its last renovations, and the other members of the management staff include three assistant managers: Rita Viola, Jonathon Berger, and Mattie Hill. The staff directly under the assistant managers is nine in number and is referred to as guest assistants. The rest of the hotel staff either answers to Shawn or one of his assistant managers.

"Oh, Shawn. I need you to give me a list of the guests who have reserved tables so I put reservation cards with names on the tables to be reserved."

"Yeah ok, Rita. You have to meet me in the office after the six o'clock pre festivities staff meeting."

"I will but I wanted to be sure you had the reservation cards so I can get someone on it."

"I'll bring them to the meeting so you can do that, but I'm still going to need you to come to my office after the meeting so we can discuss some last minute preparations Rita."

Shawn walked out of the dining hall after meeting with his assistant Rita on the last few details of the night. As he moved out into the passage that runs between the Oyster and the kitchen he moved around the staff members using the passage and stopped one of the boys pushing a large steel cart loaded with food.

The staff of the hotel wears a uniform, so as Shawn inspected the food on the trays, as other staff passed by him and the boy with the cart, he eyed his workers clothes to see that no one was being to merry. He often questioned why the owners of the hotel went so out of their way to make sure the hotel staff knew they were allowed to relax and don party gear over the holiday season. He himself did wear an unusual hat, one that was round with no bill, black, and had holiday cheer written all over it in gold letters and glitter. Shawn let the cart boy go past and continued down the passage to the end where it split in two directions. He moved out the sliding partition in the wall which was mostly invisible least you knew it was there. A lot of the old hotel's passages were designed so that only the staff members recognized they were even there, the doors to them resembling the walls they were in so much that often the newer staff would get lost in the hidden maze behind the walls of the hotel.

In his office Shawn moved toward his desk and examining the collection of piles of papers organized on the top of it, satisfied he sat down. The hotel manager office was nice to say the least. The office was larger than any of the regular rooms of the hotel, save the few rooms on the top floors that only the more important, wealthy clients could afford to rent. His style of decorating was to keep everything to a bare minimum. Shawn thought that the less distractions he let into his office the more work he got done. As he sat down tried to sink into the soft leather of his desk chair to relax some of the frustrations of his frantic last few hours Shawn noticed from across the desk the flashing red lights coming from his office phone. He knew the flashing lights could mean only one thing and that was that someone had taken the time to leave him messages on his office phone.

Any of the hotel staff knew to call Shawn on his work cell so that he could answer them right away. He had given specific instructions at each staff meeting for all calls to come to his cell, so he knew that these red lights were not from his staff but that didn't rule out one of the guests leaving him messages for personal matters they may want to discuss with him direct to his office. Many of the guests at the hotel knew Shawn not only as the manager but on a personal level, and he was well liked by many of them as a friend and confidant. So Shawn leaned across his desk tapped two of the black buttons on the base of the phone and settled back in his chair, notepad in hand, recording bits of information from the calls.

"Fuck or be Fucked!" the loud voice proclaimed. The voice continued in a quieter tone, "That said I do not see how a person or people could imagine that they need to help the world in such a way that it requires them selling innocent lives. If this were the case in the world people would be doing it already." Already Shawn tensed in his chair and covered his face with his cupped hands. "There is no threat from money kept or money spent, so there is no need to defend money to the direst extremes. If people really want to help others they would work with them to earn money, or they would give their own money and they would not steal and use prostitution to improve the conditions for the poor. I do believe people in this world may believe it to be moral to have sex if in the greater good, but I myself cannot condone prostitution for money, or prostitution in any other form." Shawn's attention now was focused entirely within the confines of his office, localized to the edge of his desk where the speaker phone continued to blare away in the ranting voice that became more familiar in each word that the speaker broadcast into the office.

"The categorical imperative in one sense or definition is that the thing to do is the thing you could best will others to do. If you were to will all others to have sex, take money, and give it to the poor then it would be the right thing to do. It would not make sense to have sex with all the rich people to give money to the poor from the perspective of the categorical imperative because it is basically a universal law theory."

After hearing this part of the recording Shawn dropped his hands into his lap, and he questioned aloud in the quite tension of the paused rant, "What kind of nut knows this stuff? And who in the hell leaves it in a voice message?"

Still the recording went on as Shawn leaned his face in close to the speaker with an intent gaze that had others been in the room might have tipped them off that Shawn was right on the edge of saying the name of the recorded caller. "Without looking at the serious possibility that the sex will create a race of homicidal maniacs that will go about their way doing whatever creates happiness in the moment, it is not that I think them wrong completely, only that I do not believe instant moral decisions with good immediate outcomes to be of the non- continuation type. It is that I believe they will build a moral code of happiness eventually that is totally and completely corrupted by past actions and decisions." Shawn leaned away from his desk. He sunk back into his leather chair and felt the softness of it. His cell phone was in his pocket and had begun to buzz and vibrate, so he reached into his pocket and silenced the cell phone. He did not pull his hand back out from his pocket, but he left it there in the cool lining of its interior cupping the cell in a cold bloodless grip.

"It seems to me simple to see that sex in any manner is not moral. It is the natural right of a person to be disliked by others, and it also is the right of a person in nature to accumulate a savings of money and properties. It is not a natural right for another person to think it moral or right, or good, to have sex with that person in the interest of taking their property to give it to the poor. It is not the right of the poor to steal from anyone, and it is not the right of another person acting in the interest of the poor to have sex with or steal from any other person. It is not a natural thing for a person to use sex to gain possessions, but it is the right of a person to protect the possessions they have gained naturally."

At this point Shawn's face had turned a bright red, and he had ruled out this message as a joke or prank. Shawn retrieved the cell phone from his pocket and as the recording went on Shawn turned in his chair toward the tall iron post of the elevated lamp behind his desk. In this position the phone recording played on behind him as he looked out of the single window behind his desk. Outside the window of his ground level office he could see the crowds gathering outside of their favorite local hangouts and the tourists to the city as they moved along the snow shoveled city sidewalk.

"I believe this true because it makes sense in nature to live and accumulate possessions and property the same as, and in the natural interest of, raising a large family. It is not in nature a requirement to have sex, and as well as sex to take the property of them to give to others without large families. If this seems naive then perhaps it is wrong to consider that in nature it's hard to have large families naturally without land and possession. To back up the view that nature is right and greedy sex is wrong I pose the question why take for another and not yourself and your own family? It is my opinion that it is because your chance of sex at all is slim if you are impoverished and without belongings. If you are to help the poor and not yourself by fucking, why not just let the poor do it themselves and reap the benefits saving yourself the moral questioning. It's probably because you cannot fuck the rich, and this is not a moral question at all, but rather one of impossibility and possibility."

With his cell in his left hand held up three inches from his face Shawn listened as the recording on his desk stopped and the ringing from his cell began. He might have just as easily delivered the message he was about to give in person, but his legs had gone cold and numb from listening to the recorded voice just as his upper limbs, torso, and face had become hot and red fueled by his anger. Shawn spoke into the small black phone in his hand at last, "Yeah, Hello?
No, it's Shawn."

"No, everything is not alright. I just got the

strangest message left in my office."

"Yes, I know that no one is supposed to leave messages here. The point is it wasn't about the hotel. I mean not really, because it wasn't really about anything. I don't know it was weird, and the voice sounded familiar, but I couldn't quite make out who it was that was calling."

"I'm tired, that's all. Look, I called you to see if you were alright. Has anything out of the ordinary happened?"

"Any strange calls or visitors maybe? What do you mean you don't know? Has there or hasn't there been anything going on I should know about. You're my guest is all, and I think that if something were going on you must tell me so I can take care of it is all. Alright, I'll be up in your room in the next fifteen minutes, but don't talk to anyone until I arrive ok. Love you."

Ch. 9

They came on their way to the city in a small red compact car. Alan in the driver's seat for an hour on a long stretch of road between his home and the city. At his last stop for gas an hour back Alan had went in to get some drinks and relieve himself, John had woke at the stop for gas. Alan got the drinks and John went back to sleep in the rear seats. Usually Alan was accompanied by a girl, but now he and

John were on their own for the first time. There were other ways it would be different Alan thought while driving as they pulled up into the large parking lot of the Red River Inn on the corner of a block of standard two- story city houses. As he pulled in, John asleep in the rear seats, Alan questioned aloud to himself why the houses looked so small and similar to the other houses on the block. It was so unique and familiar he thought when he was young, but now they were just standard normal homes to him. Alan stood up out of the car and stretched his long legs in the parking lot, cramped from the ride down, and without paying too much attention slammed the car door waking John in the backseat. Alan moved up the walk to the front door entry to the hotel, and with John behind him started knocking the bell boy about being made to wait, a process that was to take a while at least.

As Alan turned to tell John that they were just going to have to wait it out until someone showed up at the door with their tickets to the event, he realized John had gone around to the back of the hotel. Alan thought to himself how he never told John they were to arrive unannounced like they were, but was more compelled to say nothing and just follow into the back alley through the unlocked hinged gate at the side of the hotel. He knew this made John mad as he stood like he was hearing bad news, straight and with good posture, like a dog that is being given the command to sit. Funny, Alan thought that John should be so easy-going, enough so that taking a detour was no problem, but at the first sign of trouble he turns into a watchful obedient dog. They hadn't waited at the front doors for more than ten minutes to get in before John started to turn on him.

Alan Miller was a young active man in his twenties. Once a bodybuilder in high school and in college although he didn't compete any longer he still kept his body in good shape frequenting gyms and working out at home in his terra cotta mansion. He had a successful career in retail sales at a thriving suburban outlet, and he had successful friends whom he often relied on for just about anything. He was shocked to find John Handy waiting outside his home earlier in the day, and even more so by the fact that John had demanded that Alan drive him to the Red River Inn.

Alan hadn't seen John in weeks, and the last time he had seen him John was getting into an ambulance to take him to the city hospital because of a heart condition. So as Alan followed John toward the back of the hotel he questioned just what it was that John was in such a hurry to get done. Already John had given the noncompliant bellboy, a new-be if Alan had ever met one, a note with such explicit instructions on its delivery that John wouldn't even permit Alan to hear them as they were given.

74

It was John's time to enact a plan now though, and the end result was to be Alan, driving home alone as he took a pick of the hotel rooms he explained. Angry isn't the word Alan had thought as he had been the one that drove to the hotel. The two men entered the hotel's rear loading docks and immediately walked towards the delivery doors.

As John slowed down and began going into a speech about hotel security and safety, Alan looked him over as John stood towering over the smaller of the two figures. John's speech continued as the two stood not five feet from the entry point into the rear of the 18th century gothic building, and the only area of the hotel that seemed strangely deserted. Alan grew tired of the speech John had went into and tried to quiet him with gentle words of encouragement lacking any true feeling and somewhat laced with contempt for the speech. Finally, not two seconds after John announced to him that "Hotels just weren't safe", Alan had the lead pipe in his hand and was coming down on John's head like he was entering a security checkpoint after 911.

Alan had finally done it- he had put the dog to sleep, he was on his way, he would be the one parting tonight, and John he thought would take days to wake up and heal. Proud and noble Alan entered the rear doors without a fear in the world as to the overall safety of hotels.

Ch. 10

The door was locked to the hotel room. The number outside the door of the room read 700, for the room was located right at the corner of the intersection of the first two halls stretching across the seventh floor as soon as a person exited the elevator. Hotel floor plans allowed for a row of ten rooms in either direction before a means of escape was required be it a fire escape, a flight of stairs, or an elevator. This requirement met standards with the cities fire code implemented long ago. Inside room 700 there was a king size bed in the main room, and attached to the main room was a large closet, an extravagant bathroom, and a foyer at the entryway. The gothic style of the hotel permeated each and every room within its monolithic structure, and room 700 was no exception. The high walls and ceiling with the noticeable style of embedded lines were enough to send its occupants reeling if they consumed enough alcohol. The linen and drapes of the large room were decorated in blue, and the room's sole occupant for the last month had decked out the room with plenty of spare party favors, all of which were supplied either by her generous host or by one of the lower staff members of the hotel.

She sat on the large king bed staring out the open window as the snow continued to come down in modest amounts. She wore a dazzling red dress that was tight, but not so much that she could not sit and stand, too a miraculous degree. Her long hair was piled up atop her head in the latest trend with pins and what might have been considered a golden tiara, given to her by one of the staff members, which had small red letters celebrating the holidays. This woman had come to stay at the hotel at no cost to her for over a month.

Her cause for staying so long was still a mystery to most if not all of the staff members and to many of the guest assistants as well. She was an honored guest as the rumors surrounding her stay weren't at all uncommon around the hotel, and that often many women were given such long stays in the upper rooms of the hotel in off season accommodations. She was slender, but not so tall only reaching around 5'7, and her heels she wore tonight she might have reached 5'8 and a half. Her pale complexion suggested to others around the motel she was afraid of the outdoors, but the rumors suggested she was hardly allowed to leave with all of the extravagant pampering she was given by her host's undying attentions. Many of the guests and staff of the hotel upon seeing the fine lady would proclaim amongst each other as they passed with waves and giggling smiles, "That's Mr. Thawing's new girl Deb."

As she sat staring out the window watching the snow fall through the cold, dark night air Deb caught sight of her reflection as it was cast on the window. The chill of the outside night was momentarily blocked from her view as she sat in the dark hotel room. The light from the foyer as the door to the room was opened flooded through the bedroom and that light seemed to mount her reflection onto the glass of the window for the moment until she heard the door close behind her guest.

The image as she saw it was perfect. A lonely girl sitting in a room alone with a beautiful dress on her, a crown of gold around her head, and a note in her hands as they sat perched on her lap. The image she thought that would be surely perfect and just how her guest was to see her as he entered the room. She lifted the paper in her hands slightly as if to read from the lines stretching across the front of it, and she wondered if now her host too would be able to read those same lines as she.

Being unable to decide how she would look to Shawn as she sat solitary on the large blue bed she turned toward him and, she not wanting to be questioned any more by him as she had been when he had called her from his office, she began to read the poem she had received earlier that day by way of one of the newer staff members. As Shawn came into the room behind her and flicked on the light switch on the far wall illuminating the room and its towering chandelier she began to read,

"The sands of time wore on as footsteps, fleeting

as their maddened dreaming. Dreaming of shadows
and of shadows growing. Like pulling backs,
like turning necks,
With mountains breaking braided chains, we at
last heard freedom's music. As the strong and
silent, and the week, went down like missing lambs!

O' and of the despair, disbelief of fear- and yes the
ones you're seeing now, they get up, when down,
then fall, will all of it soon fall like cries cut short,
loud cries no doubt, like smiles faded, lives drown
out lives, no sounds we are the end; life makes sense
trying to recognize you.

In the minutes you've been gone the days have
slipped away, the saints have seen your choices and
the beggars dug your grave, the brave have kept on
going to the seas to meet your slaves, all of this in the
first few minutes since you has been away.

You can't see what you've left behind; I'll be with
you tomorrow. Has the time passed over your soil,
have the gardens seen your ways, do you think they
have it in them, do they want what you have gave,
your choice is to betray us, to deny us, in the time
you've been away. The days and nights we shared
together is now the line that separates living, dying,
so self-diagnosing, purposeful and efficient in all you
do set out priorities to encompass change, in entirety

what orders do you take your part is to leave all desire, to lose and desire, to be bitten. Some will quit on the ones they love. Life can hurt. Some will quit on the ones you love."

"Is that it? I mean is that what was bothering you?"

"It's different. I can't know for sure who wrote it but I think..."

"You think it was John."

"Well, yeah. I can't be sure though. I got it from one of the staff that works the front door about an hour ago, but it doesn't say who it's from and the boy who delivered it didn't know."

"Who was the bell boy? Did you get his name?"

"No not really. He just said that this was delivered and it was to come straight to me."

"Have you heard from him since?"

"No. Not from the boy, or from John. Not since he's been in the hospital. I tried to call there, to the hospital. They said that he had checked himself out. And that they were looking for him. Something about damage to his room, I think, before he left."

"Sounds like trouble Deb. Trouble we, you and I both, don't need tonight. Everything has to perfect."

Ch. 11

Midnight in the Red Oyster as a man and a woman stand near a six player Hold 'em poker game at one of the dining tables. The man is Alan and the woman is Ann, and at the table three of the players hold most of the chips, one of the three is the chip leader holding twice the chips of any other player. The man with the most chips is Shawn, to his right is seated Rita with the second largest stack of chips and to her right is seated Deb with a moderate stack of chips in front of her. As the players look on at the next hand being dealt Alan pulls Ann aside and questions her as to what appears to be happening at the table in front of them. Ann states that it appears Shawn is being aggressive and overpowering the other players with his aggression. Rita she explains is much more calculating in her game using the opportunities afforded her through Shawn's consistent bluffs to increase her chip stack. Deb she says is playing conservatively and being taken advantage of by the tougher players. Alan agrees with her conclusions and asserts that it is the aggression of the players that is the winning factor, and asks her why is it the aggressive players are winning even against the more stable skillful players.

Alan and Ann then both take seats at the table and await the next hand. As soon as Alan sits down he is treated badly at the table and is made to quickly fold his hand, Ann's luck is no better forcing her to play quietly and await a powerhouse hand. As the players sit and wait at the poker table for chances to use their time and strategies effectively, they don't realize the threat that has just been seated at the table with them. Alan is in effect the single most effective tool at winning the money from the players before him and he is sitting patiently gathering information at the table he will soon use to his advantage to neutralize his opponents, more so to stop them dead in their tracks.

As Alan sits down at the table with Ann he knows he must first look to the real problem, and that being the problem- solver himself, Shawn. Alan knows Shawn has taken hold of the table's action by abusing his power. He knows it started off hot and kept getting hotter. Shawn's attitudes reflect that of God in a way, Shawn must have complete control, he wants the other players to be happy for what they have because they have what he wants, his strategy is to win all he can without falter or flaw. Alan knows it's what happens after Shawn has taken power and started to abuse with it, he knows Shawn will not allow an individual at the table, for all must play by Shawn's rules if he is to win. Like God however Shawn's game isn't friendly enough to survive when times are hard. His strategy is to work his way up then take power just before man is at his best, he will then claim responsibility for bringing them in on the action, and with a little help a strange Utopia will form under the false constraints of Shawn's fascist ideology. Alan knows this has already happened and now it is his responsibility to bring the game around and make it right again.

The only way to bring down Shawn's game is not to attack it with any direct fatality, but instead to assemble an inside detonation, like that of a train bomb slowly entering the city. His first step is to ensure he is seated to the right of Deb the weakest player in the game, this isn't optimal strategy, it would be better to be seated in Ann's seat, but that will all come in later. Alan takes his position to his advantage by inducing the action in play to come mostly from Deb on his left , he does this by calling Deb's weak bets and folding to Deb's obvious bluffs, this loosens the strangle hold Shawn has on the game. Next he must ensure he doesn't call to often as to scare Shawn out of the game, he does this by allowing Ann's weak play to sidetrack Shawn's attention. As long as Shawn is winning Ann's chips from the position behind her he won't notice the chip stack in front of Deb growing larger. All of this leads to Rita tightening her grip on the game as we shall soon see. Alan won't allow Deb to increase her lead much, as Deb is not a strong enough player for that, she will lose too much too often and Alan won't gain any advantage through this, instead Alan will start to win back the chips from Deb, easily, and must now concentrate on Rita. Rita is a much more skilled player and sits to the right of Shawn, so if Alan is to get to Shawn his only hope is to do it through Rita. This may not be easy but it is possible.

To understand Alan's strategy concerning Rita and Deb, one must look at the types of players the two are. We already know Deb is a more modest less aggressive player than Rita, but what kind of player is Rita? Rita is a lot like Jesus, so Alan expects Rita to be more experimental than Deb, and Alan knows she wants control more than she has. Rita knows not to do anything too sudden for fear of reprise, but she also believes she will eventually win and that is the only possible outcome. Too bad she isn't too friendly, so this won't be an easy move for Alan, but with good timing and the proper moves Alan acts according to plan to bring down the Utopia Rita has her hand in, and he does it swiftly.

The next move after bringing Deb in on the action is too bankrupt her, and essentially to humiliate her, but for her own good if she wakes up and acts like an individual, perhaps making loose plays attracting the attention of Shawn, who is now becoming more angry trying to prevent the spread of individualism. With what is now starting to look like a chip lead at the table, perhaps one fourth of what the stronger players hold, Alan moves quickly under the distraction he has created with Deb. He moves in on Rita playing hands just strong enough to make the socialists mad enough to topple the weaker versions of good solid hands.

Now with a strong solid hand and all of Rita's attentions on him Alan must allow and subvert the hands of Rita. Perhaps call a bluff, perhaps just a showdown, but there is no doubting that he only has one or two tries, no more than three tries to double or triple his own stack, and to effectively cripple the stack of Rita. Once Alan has done this, maybe he had Aces, he knows that Rita won't last long in the game, usually out of anger the socialist will pack her bags and head for home calling it quits, it is essential Alan gives her no possible route for retribution, which is the socialist game, he must end any advances made by Rita after the fact thus sidelining her for the happy manufacturing plants she so well deserves.

With both Rita and Deb swept under the rug and heading for the door Alan must not hesitate in ending Shawn's game. Alan may win all the chips he may not, he may not have enough left in him after the final showdown coming with Shawn, but he has a good friend, one he believes knows right from wrong. This friend is Ann, so let's concentrate on Ann for now. He trusts Ann to know what is right, he even thinks highly of her, perhaps she is a little like him or even a little like the devil, being an devil, a studier of the metaphysics in life, a believer in what is, is, and what is not is wrong. Alan knows with other players like Ann he can easily restore balance and sanity to the game, maybe even a little happiness. He must now take the table advantage and the table image he has created to turn the entire night against Shawn if only for a moment. He begins by losing little pots to Ann and avoiding any action generated from Shawn. With this his love of life sparks in Ann and the other players and turns to bitter wrath in the frightened eyes of Shawn, who knows his day is coming. Alan allows Shawn's bitter fuel to be spent around the table one last round before moving in on the weakened plays he knows all too well. Shawn will make only one or two more bullish plays to Alan and that will be all it takes for him to have the lead and then all of Shawn's chips.

The tragedy of Alan's plays and strategies are once the fascist, the socialists, the utopian dreams are all vanquished he may have a very hard time playing to win any further- being somewhat that of the hero. Once finished with Shawn he must now make his way home, the last tyrant to retire, and as he makes his way there he may even gain a smile knowing that somewhere in the eyes of the other players there in that room he was and is, and will always be, the revolutionary and the individual.

Those who fail to learn from history are doomed to repeat it. This statement is correct, what's not correct is to assume just because you've never heard of a plan, scheme, or revolution that it must be new. Too often men don't learn from history and simply repeat the failures of the past under a disguise of a new and wonderful revolution. It's just too bad there are more Alan's in the world when you don't need them.

The Red River's lobby was jammed from wall to wall with people in the historic part of town. Inside the lobby were particular items; a chandelier, a grand piano, and spiral staircases all giving and adding to the Gothic look of that part of town. The occupants of this night, all dressed in black suits and party dresses, lingered in the opening of the great lobby with their cigars and their strong drinks. The occasional guest wandered into the street in a mad gallop to have words with a stop sign or a fluorescent ghost, so mislead by the hour and his vacant sense he'd return to the walk of the lobby. Now in what should have been a simple party with celebrating and cheer the once square room of the lobby turned, in horror of the guests, and left an empty drift in the crowd and a soon recovered elevated feel in the chest. This occasion seemed to be fit "for all and none", and so the streets would fill with the young and old returning to their lives once again. The entire night was built around the host, and the whole scene was built on holiday nights as this one in loud, cramped smoky rooms.

Once out of the larger dining hall, into the lobby and out onto the street, Alan stood alone under the artificial light of the street post sighing along with the diminishing crowd that moved past him. Alan could have been elsewhere in the night perhaps with a friend or his guests, but he stayed on the corner, for his thoughts on this event had his tongue held back and he could only marvel in awe of his circumstances. His present situation leaned heavy on his conscience, for he was the solitary inhabitant of this corner of the street, and it allowed him the greatest view of an isolated attitude. Alan in a position to argue the night away under this light, considered the folly of the event to be inconsequential as a new crowd pressed in around him, to each side pushing past him into the night, leaving him as he watched. The shadows of their figure's twisting down the broken pavement and the shapes of hooded faces tearing at the brick walls posters' advertising the holiday's events throughout the city.

The hours had grown longer as the night wore thin and the once hysteric crowd within the motel had few to remain in its arms. Alan came near to the calling of his heart and understood the meaning of things those who remained sought out so dearly. Quietly turning over in his mind now were thoughts that could wait until morning, but here they went repeating over and over claiming victory like a spider, which has paralyzed its prey. Exchanges back-and-forth from the street to the inside walls of the party's lobby echoed in the ears like a recording softly playing in the background. Only a few of the older guests of the night remained inside the hotel creating an emptier feel in what was near a riot a few hours earlier. And now those among them cheerfully reeled off about the challenging spectacle of the card game they had beheld, and left the empty street out of their sight as the doors closed.

Ch. 12

Standing-in-line, the heavy stench of starch and linen upon them, twenty staff members and three guest assistants waited at the door to Shawn's office. Their entire day rested solely on this one meeting, and had led up to this group of weary legged staff's formation outside the door waiting to be told they were allowed to leave for the night. Unique to its surroundings, set back as if out of reach of the day's work, the door to Shawn's office stood closed. An etching of promise to those who would enter through it lay on the exterior as a piece of artwork in a museum lay untouched. The tired men stood fast in their respective groups and no one dared to touch or to open the door that was in front of them. They stood and watched the door grow lonely, for as no one entered and nothing came out, it was then those who were alert in the hall began noticing the familiar urge, many learn when they are young, had settled in on them like the shadows of the door. The troubled lot had dance moves in their pockets and began to insist that the door be abandoned. Many who have danced previously in life now had the desire to feel it's free and light effects on themselves, meanwhile leaving the door alone and unguarded bothered none of them at all.

They were willing to lay it on the line in a chance attempt to escape to the dance floor for a few short minutes to use their moves without knowing the consequence of their actions. It is a well-known fact in some regions that when inhabited by the dancer the area around them suffers, the air is more polluted and the ground less clean, this is a sign to the dancer that dancing has its ups and downs. Another fact less well known to the dancer is that they themselves suffer as well as their environment. To the men and women on the dance floor that night what lay ahead for them mattered very little if at all, and whatever it might be was not what they would later tell to others as being anything that could have been expected for.

To the non-dancers that night only lies and exaggerations would be left to tell after it had all been gone over in the office behind that door with the emblem. While inside the office the discovery was made that the man behind the desk was a dancer of sorts, outside the closed door waited another line of fresh young adults slowly congregating in a game of waiting and quite reflection. Not only was the head of the office a dance enthusiast, but he was in the state of mind to dance at that very instant. This is when it all started that night on the dance floor, and what would be led along to many more places and times allowing the music lover opportunity to indulge to his pleasure if he liked.

However, once outside that office and after walking to the head of the group, Shawn's character shown in the light of the dance floor, and he left few to remain in the likeness of one such as himself. His moves and his presence left little for him to desire and in the place of his occupancy, where his two brown shoes sat firmly planted, all bets were off. In the bright lights of the dance floor some people were more conformed and governed, so many displeased by the fact that they gathered in throngs and gangs to confront an individual who had wandered to far from center of the rest. Shawn would see this and despite his warnings had to straighten things out often receiving only foul words or threats in exchange. Other downfalls for the group of dancers came on too in the form of resistors mildly claiming they only wanted to see the dance floor, and that they were not dancing that day.

Despite the bad effect of the ash swirling in the winds, and smoke leaving a scent and an oily film on the face and clothes, the thought of Shawn would return, and as many could tell you from that night on he was thought out to be a bad SOB. The night wore on and the dawn approached, and while nothing was to be gained the rest often crept back to a point of view from the dance floor- -we crept like moths that would soon surround the moonlight. Not that he was keeping track of things, but it was then that Shawn exclaimed, "Put 'em up; your times up." He had only just said it when he turned and said, "You're through, and so now; put 'em up."

Ch. 13

Behind the hotel lies the Red river known for its polluted streams and banks and its lack of aquatic life. Once the Red river was navigated by fishers and bargemen making the river the staple of the local economy, the city was founded on it. In the years since the hotel began renovations the river had lost is charm, and it began to be used as a dumping ground for chemicals and trash. The common thought among the inhabitants of the city was that what can't be seen can't be helped, but the tragedy of this mode of thought stretched beyond the banks of the once mighty river. The tragic figure of a broken and bloody man lay still in the moonlight that reflected off the dark troubled waters of the river right up the back of the hotel. The bright city lights that played in yellow and green at the front of the hotel shone red and dark along the back of the hotel. The alley way behind the hotel filled with garbage cans and bins stacked high with used party supplies was silent in the coming dawn of New Year's Day. John's body lay still in the dark red light of morning coming up over the river and fields beyond the city boundaries.

The cold wind shot down the alley and what life did survive in the harsh winter conditions moved around sparingly conserving energy and heat. A few stray cats moved around the lifeless form of the man and the pool of dark hardened blood that swam out from ignoble openings. John still in his leather coat and clothes he had worn in his escape from the hospital now used his remaining strength come back to him since the attack to fend off the rats and mice that circled him. Waving his outstretched arms across the ground in half circular motions to fend off the newest threat John tried to rise up onto his elbows to see the oncoming attack of rodents become threatened by the cats that lived behind the hotel. Thankful for his life john managed onto his knees and attempted to scoop up the nearest savior in animal form that licked at the slick pool of red blood. Thwarted by the animal John watched at the cats near him retreated back into the hiding behind the dark bins that lined the alley. Crossing his arms over his chest and trying to take a deep breath so that the oxygen in his lungs might warm him he coughed and choked on the bitter air he sucked in and watched as the vapor from his damaged body left him in a cloud of smoke. Tormented and left to sit on his knees he hugged tight across his chest and felt the warm creep in to his jacket.

Noticing the warm trickle that found its way down the side of his neck and into the fibers of his shirt John braced himself onto his hands pressing against the cold gravel and concrete. He lifted himself onto his feet, stumbling back at first and almost falling onto his ass; he regained his balance and steadied against the rear wall of the great hotel. He had fallen not ten feet from the loading ramp of the delivery door to the hotel, yet in the ten hours since he had fallen no one had come to his rescue, save the cats that lived along the banks of the river and the side streets of the city. Moving along the wall closest to where he had fell John made his way to a small flight of steps and turned his body down onto them to rest while he readjusted his mind to his current situation. He was almost dead, almost frozen in the night, and he had come close to bleeding to death as the residents of the red river ally chewed their way into his clothes.

As John sat on the cold and snow covered steps of the hotel loading dock his body began to shake and shiver. He knew it was a good thing that his body still could choose to fight the cold, but also that his body would not last much longer in the cold morning weather of January. Without much thought but a quick glance in the direction of the closed and secured rear doors of the hotel he again braced himself with one hand on the iron bar leading up the stairs and walked away from the hotel down the ill lit city alley overlooking the muddy morning river.

Part III

Ch. 14

There once was a doctor who lived in the finest house. He was a good man and he was humble. He never questioned the deeper facets of life that surrounded him and he healed the sick. This doctor often found himself dreaming of a place away from his home. That is, in the dreams this place did not seem like his home.

The place was at the edge of the water. The clear blue water that lapped at the shores, and made quite sounds, like the making of love. In this place the doctor could stare out over the waters for as long as he liked and not be disturbed. The doctor built a platform he called a dock that led out into the water twenty feet. It took him a year to complete. Once it was done the doctor would walk out over the water and stare into the blue; the blue sky and the blue water.

At times the doctor would have visitors, and they would bring him gifts. Nothing big, only little things, but the doctor was always greatly impressed by these gifts. About him, he was loved by all, he healed the sick, and he comforted the grieving. The good doctor was loved by all even nature. In nature the doctor was welcome and he could always find a friendly place to visit. The longer he lived, the doctor, the less he healed the sick, and the more he made friendly visits and was welcomed with love and adoration by all, even nature.

Soon the doctor was not called doctor by those he visited any longer, but instead he was just called friend. As a friend he grew to know the people he met in more exciting ways. Meaning that after he was no longer called the doctor, he was called friend, and he was not always treated the same as before. What would happen, still being called love, was that people would over do his visits, because they were not that of the doctor but that of the friend. He became closer and closer with the people and nature and he became the friend. The friend was never well received as the doctor, so he lied. The friend was never so well sought after, so he deceived. You see the friend was only a friend, and that was not the inviting persona he once had, but without knowing he became less and less wanted.

After a while the friend wanted more and more to be the doctor, so he tried to change. Only the friend did not know how to be a doctor anymore because he was too busy being the friend. The friend tried to tell the people to call him and he tried to tell the people to expect a visit, but it was never the same as when the doctor did it. The people reacted different toward the friend. They would not wait for him at home, and they would not take his calls. He was only a friend. The doctor inside the friend became angry after being treated so, and he swore never to act like the doctor again. Soon he was alone and isolated, and soon the people needed a doctor.

"John" she spoke, "I'm here."
"Where? I can't see you", he said.
"Right here with you. I'm here."
"Why can't I see you?"
"You can if you try. Try for me. Try to see me."
"How? Where are you? What do you look like, so I know you?"
"You know me. I'm just like you always saw."
"I know you. I'm trying to see you. Help me to see you."
"Just squeeze your eyes shut tight, and try to feel the air around you."
"Just like that, and I'll see you?"
"Yes, just like that. Now squeeze them tight like your hugging me."
"But I'm not hugging you. I don't know where you are. Why can't I see you?"
"You will. Just keep your eyes shut and feel the air around you. Try to smell the air, John; can you feel the heat in front of you?
"Maybe I can. Is that you?"

"Yes, that's me."

"What do you look like right now?"

"You what I'm like, but you can't see me- right?"

"Yeah, I know what you look like, but I can't see you. Tell me?"

"No, you're going to see me."

"No I'm not. I'll never be able to see. I don't know how."

"I'm going to show you how. Now, you know that I'm the heat in the room, the heat that isn't you. So, now I want you to feel that heat and try to see the light."

"But my eyes are shut."

"I know I want you to feel the heat, see what light you can from the room with your eyes closed."

"I can see only black."

"Is that all?"

No, I can see a little of a dark red."

"That's right John you can see your heat. Now I want you to see mine."

"Tell me how. I feel the heat in me, but you say that's not you. You say that your heat is different than my own."

"It is john. I'm not you, but I am inside you. You feel my heat, and you smell my smell. That is me. But if you want to see you have to look outside yourself, let your sense be mute and feel what's not you."

"I don't understand."

"You can smell me can't you?"

"Yes, but you said that was the heat."

"I want you to smell the heat. Not from yourself, but from me. I want you to feel the heat as it enters you from me. I want you to smell that. I want you to pretend that that smell is me moving around the room."

"You mean that as you move the smell changes. The heat that I feel is the smell that enters me."

"It enters your heat as a scent. You feel the scent as it moves within you. As I move around you, you see the heat change with my scent."

"I see you now. You don't have the shape of an object, you're only a thought."

"If I were a thought John, you could forget me."

"No I couldn't. I love you."

"I'm here with you."

"Yes. I know. I can see your love."

"I am your love"

"You're inside my heart. Moving me and opening my eyes."

"I love you."

"I love you...I want to know you."

"We will know each other."

"And...Where are you?"

"See me, see me."

"I see you, but bow I want to use my eyes. Tell me how."

"Your eyes will let you see me, let you know me, but

you have to be objective. You have to accept that I'm something other than you."

"I can. I trust you, to love you."

"Within your heart you have a scent. You have captured my form inside yourself. You can reach out and touch me, but then you have to see me."

"I have to see you."

"I want you to open your eyes."

"Will I be cold?"

"No. You won't be cold. You will still have the heat. Only now you have to use that heat to see."

"I want to see, but I don't want to lose you, I don't want to open my eyes."

"It's ok; nothing I'm doing is going to hurt you here."

"I'm opening my eyes to you."

"I see the way I always have without ever having opened my eyes."

"I see the black void in which I exist. I see the warm red whispering fan of your breath moving the embers of my heart."

I move my body and the embers respond with excitement. They and I consume you."

"You are my sight. You are the burning glory of my efforts. Like a flaming angel, like dragon's breath. Like a lit furnace taking human form and glowing red hot in the night air you stand."

"I watch as you lift off the ground, and I promise myself not to let you fly to high. It is too late you are in the clouds. I am scared the cold clouds choke my breath as I watch you."

"Please come down out of the sky. I can't feel the warmth any more, and I am afraid. My heart pounds in my chest, like fear. But I only want my breath back, the warm breath I have."

"While you float there in the clouds you take strange shapes and colors. I hear you calling to me only the sound of your voice is terrifying to me. I am trapped in the clouds without breath. Please come back to earth, let me feel my chest."

You beauty is unimaginable as you float and move across the sky. I only wish that the cold feeling of your coming down was less real. You move slowly too slowly while you are away. I can barely hear, and that scares me as well. I prefer the thunder of the sky to your figure burning in my mind."

"As you come near me, and me to you, I see the blackened fire of my heart explode into a blue cloud. The raincloud of my mind, it is you."

My darling, my treasure, you are the golden beam of the heavens, but you come to me as a blue cloud moving in a white gown."

"You are the drops of rain as they hit my face and tear down my skin. Oh I feel the pleasure of the gods as I watch you soar toward me. No mortal, but the movement of the heavens, a star burning in the whitest circle approaches my color."

"I am left standing on the green earth of the dreamiest

space cloud, and your majestic blue surrounds and encompassed my eternal form as I float in heaven enchanted by your grace."

"I fall a million miles to the gray cold stone, the tallest cliff, the highest mountain."

"You come at me from the heavens as if the crushing waves of the great blue ocean."

"Consume me, again and again, like the beating of my heart. Never let the pounding cease until the vision disappears."

"Leave me again and again, crush me with your power, your might, your grace."

I am the space heaven; I am the blackest cloud glowing under the moonlight."

"I am under your spell, and with me you will remain forever unblemished."

"In your waters the golden light melts through the surface. Attacking at my base, attacking my foundations; The light that I cast out, in this shroud of forest, this overhanging dense den of woods, this covering of my overhanging rocky cliffs. "

You subvert me you destroy me, you let the heavens in. The light shines across your surface and pulls at me, breaking pieces of me away to swim across your long golden tresses. I am Jason, I will not live long. I promise."

I've just woken up. I lay still in my bed and without thought open and close my eyes. I know the light from the window above my head hurts my eyes as it creeps into my mind illuminating the dark images from my sleep. The images that were to remain unseen take form in my mind and I close my eyes to block out the dreadful light that invades my mind. After a few minutes the violent storms within my head break apart and cast off the light from the images letting them go back to sleep within me.

Again I open my eyes this time willing out the light that still fills my room. I've always done this and sometimes I've let this go on for days at a time. Closing my eyes and opening them, just to close them again. The rainbow of colors from the world, from the sun with its red and blue, and green terrifies me. I let the color fill me only to dispose of it. I am like a child learning to walk each day, only a child would learn to overcome the physical obstacles in his way to learn to walk, such as the carpet, a dog, or a table. I have to learn to walk around the colors that try to invade my path. I mean the yellow that flies above my head, the red that shines at the door inviting me through two steps ahead of my pace; an 'impossibility' if you think about it. I avoid the blue that cries in the cup that wishes me to swallow it up. I move myself with the grace and care of a mother carefully picking up the colors that swarm throughout the world, the objects of this world all must move with me, and I with them.

Only today as I play this game with the world

in which I live I move slower more cautious, and with an unease that spells out disappointment, and I hear the colors cry out because we are not in step with yesterday. I wander down the hall from the bedroom and notice my slippers are not on my feet, now instead they are walking behind me, following me down the hall. The sound of my bare feet whispers to me that the floor is too cold and I must wait for the slippers at my heels to join me at the entrance to the next room, also unfamiliar.

I realize that this place is not my home, but it is a home. I wait at the door as the wood spills around me, and I think will my cousins in Oregon be worried that I am taking too long to return. Will they miss me? My blue fuzzy slippers behind me never catch up to me and I fall forward into the kitchen, why am I in the kitchen. I crawl forward on my knees, my hands before me pushing away at the light and dragging me behind them. I reach a new tree. This tree spells out to me that he was broken to pieces years ago. He tells me his years in a broken language and he stands so still. Are you afraid here tree, I am. When will the rain come, to fall in tears throughout my mouth, oh worrisome rain come to me and make the river man rise up from the streets.

Not too long ago I carried myself down the river to be one with the sun, but I couldn't see you as you passed, but still I walked and I heard you crying.

Did I scare you? I meant only to awaken you to me, so that you would not hit me anymore. I have run miles. Since that day at the river I awoke to see the still water stopped and tranquil, in a rush of light did the waters move and carry me away from that tallest of stones. I have run miles since that day. I awake hear and now I can hear the river speaking to me that the light has caught at his hooks and placed him far away.

Where am I now? Why am I all wet, I know that the water moves down my front, and the blood is gone from my neck. O holy sink that fills my cup, may you never run dry so long as I live. Whose house is this and why don't the cups run to me and call me father here. Please brother, brother plate let me build my castle and do not be so mad at me, I can't understand you when you're mad. I am at Alan's house. I broke in last night through a window. I smashed that window and it cried. I stopped to cry with him, but the blood moved down to my arms, o lonely neck you never where what they wanted were you.

This place is different than before, it is empty, so is my stomach, oh lonely plate, master of this house tell me of you victory and let the waters run beside your burning lake. The river never runs when it is a lake. I woke up at Alan's and here I am at his table eating my breakfast. I think she's pregnant; what am I to do? What I always do. I will go and ask for the little things that they are eager to give me; they love to break the stones that are there hearts. I will watch and listen as the birds chirp over their heads. They love the birds. I can climb a tree but I can't tell what a bird is. Ill laugh to loud, and then they won't break the stones, the birds will fly from threes and I will go back home to the sounds of melting hearts. Hearts that must be melted so when I return they will have new forms; and make new sounds when they break apart. I am the eagle, and you and you and you are my sparrows. Feed me not, light, but feed me flesh therefore I will not die. It is the middle of the day, but I will find you.

Even in the heavens my face can see you, you little specks of darkness, you there are the sparks that light my way. Lead me little doves and I will fly away. I can soar higher and higher until you are out of my sight. You will not see me I will fly so high, and then until I break at the sun and fall from the heaves in a rainbow of forbidden colors will I join you and there you will interpret my dreams, but that is when you will start to fear me and turn that light against me.

I give chase but you know my power will when I close my eyes. I will move up the greatest mountains, down the coldest banks. The purest waters flow backwards so that when you find them they will be dirty. This is a curse on you. I live in the tree. I live on the mountain. The rain here loves its children. The rain falls into the sky, and it is beautiful to see.

Ch. 15

Policewoman, "Hello, you've reached the Central City Police Headquarters. If this is an emergency please hang up and dial 911. Otherwise how may I assist you?"

"Yeah, hi, my name is John Handy. I'm calling to report a crime. Actually I'm calling to report a whole list of crimes, crimes committed against me, crimes that I'll testify to in a court of law."

"Ok. Sir what's going on? Are you in danger and what's your location? Do we need to send an officer in a squad car?"

"Listen to me. It's not me that's in danger, at least not at the moment, or at least not that I'm sure of, but what's important is my girlfriend is being held by people, people that won't let me see her. These people are criminals and I demand that someone do something. I've tried and they used violence against me."

Policewoman, "Sir, what's your girlfriend's name, and where is she at the present."

"Her name is Debbie, and she's being held at the Red River Inn, but I'm not sure if it's against her will, like a kidnaping, or if she's just there being brainwashed. I need help! They won't let me see her."

The Policewoman says, "The Red River? Sir, who is it that you claim used violence in keeping you away from your friend Deb."

"The entire hotel is infested with criminals. Every last one of them is in on some sort of game. A game their not talking to outsiders about. I was there a few days ago and was attacked. I can't be sure who my attacker was because he jumped me from behind, but I know they were working for the hotel. The entire affair I was there to enjoy with my girlfriend was set up by the manager. His name is Shawn Thawing, but that's not it, one of Shawn's own friends he took me there and he had to of seen me being attacked, because he was right there. They might have got him too, I don't know I haven't seen him and he hasn't been home since."

Policewoman, "What's his name John."

"His name is Alan Miller."

Policewoman, "I need you to stay calm sir. I'm going to send a squad car to the hotel to talk with Mr. Thawing, and I want you to give me the address to this Alan Miller's house so I can send an officer to check in on the property. John I need you to give me your location so we can send a detective over to ask you some further questions and just to make sure you're alright, ok."

"That's good. That's all I'm asking for here."

109

At the entrance way to the park the cars all line the streets and there is an empty spot at the corner of the large parking lot. John pulls the car into the empty spot and gets out of the car. His shoes are brown and ragged as are the rest of his cloths. His jeans are torn and blood stained. His favorite leather jacket is torn and the black color of the damned thing is set off by the dark red smears of dried blood.

John tries to wipe at his clothes and jacket to look more presentable, but it is an act more of habit than of desire. The park closes in about an hour and as John walks towards the open field ahead of him many of the people that have enjoyed the sunny day there already are leaving. As the people walk past John as he enters he is sure they assume him to be a vagrant looking for a place to sleep, but no one speaks to him in any way that he can understand. He is not looking for a place to sleep of course; he is looking for a man. John has a plan and this man is the key to it all.

John met this man only once from a distance. It was the day that he allowed himself to go to the park with Debbie. Alan and Anna had brought them here and Alan had known this man. As John approaches the area that he remembered coming to that day he sees the man's booth. A flower booth set back against the tree line on the south side of the park. A place that people come and go and if the man is lucky they stop to fall in love and to prove it they buy his flowers.

But flowers are not all the man sells from his booth, as John knows from that last day here when Alan approached the man for marijuana, weed. They sun is beginning to go down in the western sky and the shadows from the trees are stretching off longer and longer as John makes his way toward a park bench a few feet from the vendor.

Isolated couples and small groups of people wander out of the park coming near to the booth and the man within politely offers up his goods for sale. One couple, that just came from the north trail of the hilly side of the park, stop to talk to the man. He is tall and well built. A large man with dark-black hair and nice features, his skin is dark and he speaks with an accent. He is exuberant in his gestures as he tries to convince the couple that his flowers are the perfect end to a day in the park.

The man of the couple moves his head in close over the counter as he looks at the flowers. The tall Indian moves around in the back of the shop handling the flowers explaining each variety by name and fragrance, but the man, a young jovial man in matching winter colors to his girl with him, snickers to the Indian about a different sort of flower that might be sold. John overhears the young man's question and realizes that his presence either must be made more pronounced or be made to be invisible.

John stands up from the bench, looking fully like a vagrant by this time, and moves to stand at the corner outside the booth. The moon is low in the sky over the trail the couple has come off from, and the sun is continuing to sink lower, and lower in the horizon glowing red in the dusk. The Indian seems unfamiliar with the question and moves his hand up from a vase full of purple flowers. He runs his hand through his bark hair and leaves it there atop his head as if to gesture with his elbow if the woman with the man too is in search of the weed.

The young man smiles to her and offers a wad of money to the Indian man, but John has crept in too close and all are aware of his presence there at the booth now so to ease the tension John too takes out a wad of money as he gestures over the counter of the shop. The Indian man is satisfied that all present parties want this particular variety he has and reaches under the counter returning with a black box, a safety box, which he lays on his counter before the three now standing in the blue light of the on setting night.

"Thank you" as the lid snapped shut.

Ch. 16

As I wander through the alley behind the old hotel I realize that I am alone. No sounds come from around me, but the ancient highways that surround all leaves trail of dust that rise into the air. The sun

112

shines down over the old hotel through the dirt and dust rose high above it; they leave the color of the sun burnt and dry as though the trails of red smoke rise into the heavens, stretching forth unto the sun. There at the sun the trail ends and the bur begins. It engulfs the scraps of life and sends down the rainbow of color, only the color is red. The hotel is illuminated and quite, only the sound of burning surrounds it. I walk through the smoke and fire towards the rear entry. The stains of my blood no longer litter the ground, but they have turned to red, to fire, rising in the sky and circling the streets and highways. The river behind me, over my shoulder gleams bright, blue water flows beneath its tepid waves. The trunks of fallen soldiers- fallen trees- turn and swirl in the waters of the river, forbidding me to come this far. The lives of the past haunt this open stretch of forgotten city, and plead with me to go back, to follow their broken limbs. I cannot.

I enter through the double doors after I have climbed the stairs. Now I am inside the chest of the great giant. I will not hurt you here, she cries. I am astonished with my appetite. I yearn not for sleep; I trudge on past the men in white. I come from the great city to enter into the heart of it all, and yet I find I am alone still here within your walls. I wear my tattered clothes and my torn jacket, but you don't notice that. I move behind the walls, as I climb the stairs of the men and women residing here. I brought a gift to give my love if only she accepts me. I know I am near the heart of the hotel for I can smell my love. She moves within the confines of this place, she is a dove. She has flown in one of the open windows and I can hear her call. She is looking to escape and if only I reach her soft cooing first, my gift will be her favorite. I am not afraid here, but I feel the cold.

The cold you speak of in the words you give to me, as if they can compare to the gift I have brought to give my love. She hates the cold, and I love her, she will be mine again. I will reach her I think to myself as I walk these halls. Your painted faces leaking down your dull white coats. I should have e brought some papers or a pipe so that the gift will be enjoyed, but I don't care you sold me love and I oblige by turning to one with the sky I light the remnant of a joint as I walk down the hall, and now you notice me as I move.

You must enjoy my walk, the gift of love drifts sleepily behind me. I am becoming. You fall in step with the beats of my heart, and with you behind me I move faster, I am going to my love. Love exists in all things here within this great beast. I move effortlessly across the flooring and up the steps, I bend around the corners of the fragments of bones, and you fall away behind me with the smoke. I let you rise into the sky, keep rising I say and you will meet the sun, your burn may start and then you to will wish to return to your loves. Where is my love, where is she. I find the scent of the hunting dog has lived within this place for centuries. Yet I do not have the power of my sense I can borrow his, the dog, I can smell you in your perfume.

I can tell the way they move the words they speak, the cold spells out your name on the closed window, write out your heart. The dove is perched in the corner of the room I hear her cooing; the heartbeat of the beast moves faster. Where is she? Where is my love? I can feel the cold; I can read the writing of her heart. The dove flies into the hallway, her whiteners breathes of chill morning air. The lights flicker in the beating of her wings. I have followed you here; I have just only now found you my deer. The coldest cause of my mind says to let go of the joint in my hand, pinched between my fingers, the fire has gone out, the last plume of it filters through the air with the breath of the burning of the skin of my fingers.

The studio is a set up in the basement of the building. It's got all the equipment needed to record a studio album. It only takes up the space of the far corner near the rear of the concrete labyrinth. Corner, but extra equipment like cases and storage unit not to mention cables and wiring harness take up the rest of the rear wall of the basement. The studio is something of its own self-contained room. Almost

115

like a tiny house in the far rear, it's where the likes of many, if not all, of the city's best musicians have recorded. It has its own soundproofed enclosure, has a window for communication between the ones in the booth and the ones behind the recording mixers. There is hundreds of thousands of dollars inside the mixing console. Heaps upon heaps of expensive black boxes, with slides, and red and green lights strewn across their tops.

On the other side of the window, in the recording booth, there are thousands of dollars more worth of equipment. Microphones are hanging from the top of the booth, a drum set is a permanent resident of the booth even when the artist inside likes his beats to come from a drum machine or synthesizer. There are several guitars, much like you'd expect in a country man gun rack, the guitars come in all shapes and sizes, six string leads and four string bases. The most distant looking piece of equipment within the booth is the keyboard synthesizer; it just looks alien next to the more traditional pieces. The studio has produced countless underground records and hits that have not only traveled their course in the head shops, secondhand stores, and record stores, but in and out of the radio stations throughout the city for the past three decades.

John's footsteps echo across the expanse of the basement as he walks to the back corner containing the studio. For being the most expensive part of the hotel it oddly is the one piece of the place that is left unprotected and unlocked, sort of a promising exit to the myriad of doomed entrances. The studio sits back as far as one could imagine but the lights are on at all times. The pleasure never stops. John approaches the door to the recording booth; the silent enclosure is lit with bright lights and covered in tan brown padded materials giving the light the same off color. John removes his jacket at the door and leaves it bundled up beside as he enters the enclosure. He stands within the atmosphere of the booth like a giant, no more less than a man. He wears only his dirty blue jeans and white t- shirt other than his black shoes.

He lifts the red, white and blue guitar from off the rack of twenty, and reaches out to the switch on the connecting amplifier. He throws the switch and the red eyes of the dragon glare forth. He stands and faces the open door to the booth, and again he reaches to the amplifier this time adjusting the volume by turning the knob to its maximum position. The whine of electricity growls in a dull hum from out of the twin set of twenty inch speakers.

John stands with his feet in black shoes shoulder width apart. He bends his knees slightly, and he pushes forward his crotch and abdomen, pressing himself against the cold body of the electric guitar. He runs his hands across the smooth skin of the tool he holds and with his fingers he feels out the

117

knobs and buttons of the cold frame. He turns it on. "Burrrrrr" escapes the speakers behind him. He adjusts the tone and volume of the buzzing to his liking and with his head held low over his chest he closes his eyes. He absorbs the sounds from around him; he swallows up the static from out of the air. He runs the music now, not the control booth.

John raises his left hand to the neck of the guitar and places his fingers into position. He moves his right hand over the stings of the guitar just barely above them not quite touching the strings. He moves his right hand up and down before the strings as he sways his head, eyes closed. At last he lifts his hand up over the guitar and his skeleton tightens as if to say this is the moment, now comes the sound. As he drops his hand and the pick between his fingers goes down hitting strings he raises his head to the where the sounds should flood forth around him, but instead he looks straight ahead his eyes fixed before him into the darkness of the basement. The lights go off around him, and no sound escapes the speakers real or otherwise imaginary.

"Who's there?" John belts out into the dark. The stillness of the basement is interrupted by the bright beams of light from two flashlights as they scan the darkness for signs of life.

"Come out with your hands up!" a voice screams. "This is the City Police. We know you're in there!"

John's face is flooded with the blood of embarrassment as he removes the guitar strap from around his neck and places the instrument on the ground. "I'm unarmed. I'm coming out just don't shoot." He walks out of the booth into the beam of the shaking lights knowing at each one an officer of the law is coming towards him.

"Put your hands over your head, and don't move. John Handy you're under arrest."

"Ok, what did I do?"

"For starters you're trespassing."

"I know the owners of this establishment. You can call them if you like."

"Too late." The two officers were upon John; one held the beam of his flashlight straight into John's face as the other officer removed each of John's hand from atop his head and placed them into handcuffs. "The hotel manager told us we would find you here. What do you know about a fire at the City Hospital Mr. Handy?"

"I can't believe this shit. A fire, what fire? You mean there was a real fire?"

"Sir you have the right to remain silent. Anything you say can and will be used against you in a court of law. Do you understand this?"

"Yes. What charges are you holding me on?"

"We just want to take you back to the station and ask you some questions, and if you're lucky no one will press any charges against you than we'll let you go. Ok sir, let's move." The officer with the flashlight turned toward the staircase to the far of the basement as the other officer escorted John, with his hands behind his back cuffed, to the exit.

As the three of them walked out of the basement up the stairs John kept his head down low and mumbled to the officer behind his back, "I want to call my lawyer. I want to talk to Shawn Thawing as well, and I need to see Deb. Can I do that, please?

The police officer replied over John's shoulder in a gruff tone, "We'll get it all taken care of at the station sir, so don't you worry about a thing Mr. Rock star."

Ch. 17

"Sir, do you know why we asked you to come in and talk to us here today?" The detective sat in the plain black office chair at the head of the brown collapsible table within the interrogation room of the City Police Downtown Headquarters.

"No, not really I mean. I know it has something to do with John Handy, that's all." The man spoke from his seat at the middle of the table on the far side of the room away from the two way mirror. He looked over at the mirror as he answered and then to the detective in his seat.

The detective grinned and folded his hands before him on the table top. He wore his best grey suit with a black tie that matched the color of his hair and mustache. "We called you in because this fellow John has told us that you attacked him last weekend at a hotel party. He said you two were entering through the back doors when you came up behind him and assailed him. Is that true sir?"

The man looked at the officer with an air of grave disbelief and said, "No! Absolutely not. We were together that night at the hotel. He just showed up at my house out of the blue and invited himself to come along with me as I was on my way to the party, but I never hit him. When we got to the hotel we didn't have our tickets, so I told the bell boy we, John and I, were friends of the manager Shawn Thawing. The bell boy wouldn't let us in so we went around back because Shawn had told me how to get in the building after hours if I ever wanted to go down to the studio with friends."

"Ok sir, can I call you Alan? So you were with John the night of the party, but what happened and why does he claim you attacked him?"

"He fell! That's what happened. I saw him fall on the ice of the loading dock and he tumbled down the stairs. I went inside to get help. I found a couple of staff members that said they would go get him and call an ambulance. I thought they did that's why I didn't go back for him. Some things wrong with that guy John, my neighbors have been leaving messages that he's been hanging around my house

121

while I'm not there."

"So he fell, and you never hit him. If that is the case than I'm going to need the names of the men you requested help out this John character. If they back up your story then there isn't much else we can do. As for whether or not he's been to your house, we can arrange for a restraining order if you like."

"Do you really think that necessary Detective. I mean he hasn't really hurt anyone has he?"

"Technically no, but this isn't the first time he's implicated you in a crime either. He called before and gave us a story about a kidnaping. He seemed to think you and Shawn Thawing were in some sort of kidnaping ring, something about a girl named Ann and one named Deb. We already talked to Thawing about all this and he's clueless. We haven't found any traces of anyone named Ann or Deb being listed missing persons, and nothing was on the register at the Red River so we're writing this John guy and his whole story off as him being a nut."

"He's been really different over the past few months, that's for sure."

I have been locked in this cell for the last two days of my life. A six foot by twelve foot cell with concrete floor and walls. My only entrance, or exit in this is a row of iron bars that are out of my control. I am a prisoner here, alone with only a bunk with a one inch high mattress and an iron toilet. They put me here against my wishes. I was only trying to help the ones I love, and that's more than a lot of men do every day. I was sentenced to stay here, I have no choice. My only crime, at least the one I'm aware of, is in loving my friends, loving my lovers. I know that by the time I am allowed to leave it will be too late, but I am imprisoned here all the same.

The time passes by here differently than in the world I have always known. I can no longer walk down the street. I cannot go to the park on a Sunday. All I can do is move around this cell and try to occupy time, but the time is different here. I have been here only a few days, but already I have fallen asleep inside. My mind wanders the world I have known forever and always will know in my heart, only now my heart is broken. Time is broken too inside my heart. It only takes a minute to feel a lifetime of grief explode and collapse like a star in space in this place. I have felt the heavens change many times already.

Each time I lay down, each time I get up, the heavens change. I feel my chest rise and fall in monotony, interrupted by the shifts in time. I learn to breathe again each time this happens. I learn alone, without any teacher to lead me, with no one to be with me. I have learned to die, as I live. My life from before has entered into this cell only to die each time it comes.

I'm dying and I know it. I feel the blood fill

my lungs when I breathe in the shards of the broken. I feel the tearing in my stomach where once was only twisting. I release my mind from this place, but my mind captures it every second I exist in it. It moves within me now, it moves within the walls, around the bars, and it slithers away like a serpent that is reaching out for home. I know the empty now, and I know the hurt. I know that Ann is gone and she is not ever coming back. I know somewhere outside these walls Shawn is with Deb and he is telling her lies. Lies that eat away at her like a poison made to kill.

He wins her over, and over, and over. Each time she resist he forces a new thought down upon her. He is playing God with her, and she feels the devil, she writhes under his control. The lies she is being fed will reverse her growth as a human. Her every part and piece will grow small. She will become a fairy. She will not be a human once he is done. He is not God, he is the devil. He is the devil that led me down the path to condemnation.

I once was close to living, outside these walls, but now my life that wants to grow, that wanted, shrinks under the evils of a man not of my peace. A man that knows no peace. That man knows only sin and destruction. I followed along in his ways for far too long. It has cost me everything. By the time tomorrow comes he will be inside her, he will of gotten rid of her already before she parts with her body. I will never have that chance.

124

I think of chances here. I think of time. I think of all the ways that things could have been different only had I not been locked here in this bed. If only. I know that my life was never perfect, and that I only wanted then, but I want now. Too much has already happened. I have turned bad so quickly. I am sorry all I ever wanted was to escape myself and this chill. If the February air could but for a moment live in the warmest gust of June, it would have lived a million years.

The City Police Downtown Headquarters is located in the older district of town. Much like many of the old high rise buildings in the surrounding blocks the Headquarters is of old brick and mortar design, much in need of refurbishing. The Headquarters is one of the few single story buildings in the area, and it sits squarely facing 89th street. The long walk to its doors is done briskly from either the front, with parking along the busy street or from the parking lot to the side used mostly by the officers in the work around the clock.

Today on a usual cold February morning in the week day a tall skinny woman dressed in the warmest of fashion walks up the walk in front of the Headquarters to the wide front doors. As she walks the sounds of the street fade out as the sounds of her tall black boots ring along the concrete path. She opens the right door with her left hand, fitted snugly

125

in a cotton glove, blue matching her scarf and hat, and she swings the door wide as her body's frame slides into the pale amber light that glows within the Headquarters front office. Shaking off the cold from her long black overcoat she walks toward the officer on duty stationed behind the front desk, an elevated platform much like a courtroom, and she removes her gloves pocketing them as the officer looks down at her. The officer, also a woman, offers her a cold stare of question, and intrigue, much like many of her counterparts, other officers, mostly male, and looks back down at the desktop she works at.

The woman has reached the desk and stands a few feet back so as to alert the female officer of her arrival and intent, the woman removes her hat and placing it into her bag exposes her long black hair stretched straight and neat down her back. She reaches into her purse there and extracts a leather bound billfold of the long and black persuasion. The officer at the desk reaches out her hand down toward the woman without lifting her head from her work or the pen she holds from the papers sitting atop the desk. The woman hands the officer an identification card from the purse and waits for the officer's attention.

"Mrs. Thawing. Nice Photo. How can I be of service to you this fine day Ma'am." the officer says as she focuses on her guest.

"I'm here to see to the release of one John

Handy. He is a friend of my husband." The woman speaks to the officer while adjusting her billfold back into her bag.

"A friend of your husband? Why doesn't your husband come in? Do you know the man?"

"I do. My husband has decided to go an excursion with a female friend of Mr. Handy, and I want to see him released into my custody."

"Why would you want to do a thing like that for a man that has just run off on you?"

"It's important I see John Handy. I need to speak with him in private."

"Well the judge has set bail on your Mr. Handy. Do you wish to post bail on his behalf Mrs. Thawing?"

"Yes."

"Bail is set at 10,000 dollars. To post bail you need to pay 10%, that's going to be 1,000 dollars."

"Ok, yes I want to post his bail."

"Alright, Mrs. Thawing."

"You need to go down this hall here to your left to the last door on the right. They will take the set bail amount from you and give you a receipt. I need you to bring that receipt back here to this desk and then we can release Mr. Handy into your custody, but remember if he doesn't show up for his court date all funds given in this transaction will be kept by the city. Do you understand what I've told you?"

"Yes. I'll be back with the receipt. Thank

you." She turns and walks down the hall to the door she was instructed to enter while the officer picks up the phone at her desks and requests the inmate John Handy be brought from his cell to the front office of the headquarters.

Ch. 18

At his cell John is lying on his bed in silence, but he is not quite asleep. A large male officer, with a bald head and bulging muscles arrives at the cell doors with a lark set of iron keys. The officer inserts the proper key into the cell door and the bars roll back and to the side leaving the entryway to the cell exposed. The officer implores John to remove anything that is in his belongs from the cell and to follow down the corridor out of the inmate's secured area. John gets off the bed and puts on his shoes after which he steps out of his cell and the officer begins to move toward the steel door at the end of the corridor. In the front waiting area of the headquarters John notices the beautiful dark haired woman standing in front of the desk as Shawn's wife but he does not call out to her by her name. He is released into her custody by the jailers and he and the woman exit the building together. She holds the door for him as he walks into the city's sunlight momentarily blinded and confused by the change.

I am home, at least I am not held captive. But this is not my home. This woman has released me, and she has brought me into her home. I have been here before though, for I know this place as Shawn's. He isn't here, only his wife and I are here and she is in the kitchen brewing tea. She says it's too cold out. She gave me clothes to put on; I think they are Shawn's. The clothes lie on the sofa, I sit here in the front room with Shawn's clothes laid out beside me as if Shawn was here talking to me but he has disappeared and only his clothes remain. I feel disoriented, and I want to drink the hot tea that this woman is preparing for us.

I stand from out of my seat and I lean over the sofa, it's as if I am whispering into Shawn's ear to give him one last goodbye, but instead I pick him up and carry him with me into his bedroom, our bedroom. I remove my clothes as he sits on the bed watching me, he waits. I leave him in my underwear and I step softly into the adjoining bathroom. My feet are tender and sore, I can only feel half my toes and my arches are killing me. I turn on the hot water in the shower and wait for the steam to envelop the bathroom. In a shroud of mist I am naked. I move under the water as it hits my face I close my eyes.

I think the water here is very warm because I know it is February. I know that some force is at work deep beneath the ground, and that it has favored me with blissful intent. My face pushes back the

129

waters from my body- it does this so that I will not drown. The water does not rise around my ankles, the rest my hair absorbs. The pools at my feet as I stand feel the glow of red; it is my blood warming the water now.

I am alive. The redness disappears from at my feet and the skin of my body moves me in higher directions. I open my eyes and see the doves as they fly past me they swarm above my head from the tallest tree that grows just above me. I am warm. I wait for the doves to land, to make noise- I raise my arms in excitement.

The water dies. It dries up, and takes the doves with it, but new doves are replaced in her eyes. She has followed me under the waterfall and the light from her body creates rainbows in the mist of the forest. I feel her hands touching me. I close my eyes for a moment and again I see the white doves before me. Touching me my skin makes noise- it is the sounds of doves. We escape with our arms over our heads from the waterfall, and we fall beside the ocean.

The oceans water are not tranquil, they move and swell, with the rhythms of our two bodies fallen together. We are on the beach we are cover in sand, just like we always are, but this time the sand does not stick to our skin. We are much too polite, and the sand lets go of us so as not to offend. We enter each other and the doves change colors. No longer white

130

they are the color of her skin, her dark brown native skin. She melts over me as we slide into the ocean, the sand rolling beneath us and the waves rolling over us. We are at union- we become one within the sea. The color of our bodies ends, and the unity of our souls begins. Her mind fills the cracks in mine. My skin fills the vacuum in hers.

I move my arms before me. I see them with my eyes, yet they are not the color of my skin. I know this isn't real. It's too good here. I love being here. I move my arms at the shapes before me and they turn to crystal. I shake my fists at the air and the shadows move around me. I win at all costs. I compromise my inner wishes, my inner sanctuary in order to overcome my fears.

Like a wave breaking on the shore. No, like a stone on the beach that wishes to know the ocean. I break in pieces to travel in the currents. I learn your ways, and I see myself becoming smaller. I look to the walls of earth that line the bottoms, and I crawl across the deep expanse that stretches out for miles. I lay hold of the rock as it forms at the perfect moment. It becomes a shape, but I do not see the shape. I become a part of that shape. I am the stone at the bottom. I do not know that I am a stone.

Instead I am what I believe I am. I am home, I am after the end. I am only what you call me, what you know me to be, yet I am myself still only you no longer know me. I was a stone upon the beach, one that was looked upon. I fell apart to meet the seas, you did not understand me. I crawled across the ocean floors and settled on the bottom. I became the bottom. I am the name of things you called, but the things you never called me.

Now I met the hottest drifts of sea and rock and lava. I burned into a perfect shape and then I left the bottom. I am what was, what's never been. I see myself from within. You see me as tomorrow. I rise above the oceans waves and seat myself besides you. Now I sit again a rock the same as before and yet you will not call my name, I am forevermore. You seem to have forgotten me, and so I am distracted I think instead of sitting here, I'll lie deep in the waves. Perhaps then you will remember me, and never call me salt again.

Love Unimpaired.

By AJ Ireyes

An Impaired Love:

Get Love, Unimpaired.

Table of Contents

Foreword

This book is going to make you popular, almost too popular, so be careful as you deal with its subject matter. Going into this it may be easy to think this material won't help you get women, that its just not going to happen, but trust me it will and if you act like it isn't it will just make it worse. This book is not written by a pick up artist who went to the bars every night trying to learn how to pick up drunk chicks.

The material you find in this book is written by a guy who met girls at all hours of the day, or night, and went from being a nobody to a local legend. Granted a lot of the time girls were there looking for sex, but more times than not these girls were approached sober and just trying to have a good time. The methods inside this book are complex, but not in practice.

The time it takes for you to think about the material presented within is the time it takes to score with the ladies. Good luck on your journey to legend status, just follow the material and try to keep an open mind.

There are a lot of NLP, Self-help, hypnotism, and psychology hints in the material- but I assure you that just because this book is presented in more of a study format that doesn't mean you won't be prepared to pick up chicks and to be hit on by hot women.

The real secrets in this book are encoded in the stories of three individuals, but don't worry each story is broken down into its component parts, and afterwards

there is good discussion on the
underlying principles of why these
tactics are so effective- and they
are effective.

As of right now you have 'Game'

I was never the awkward kid
that never got girls, at first. At
first, I was the aggressive kid who
just took whatever he wanted and got
away with it just fine. The problem
I encountered was that as my tastes
in women grew I started packing on
baggage. Now please understand I
don't mean anything bad by saying
baggage, its just that the more
women I picked up the more guy
friends started to follow along- the
problem was I wasn't a guru and had
no time to even consider that these

guys wanted help with the ladies. I never considered they wanted help, so what did I do? I mistakenly started taking advice from some so called pick up artists and I transferred this info to the rear, I started packing baggage just like the average pick up artist is bound to do.

The main focus of my energies in teaching you these methods comes from a sort of empathy for my readers. To explain I must remind the reader that I was very popular from the get go, it was just that I quickly got bogged down by the world. The tricks and methods I give

here are based a lot on being
natural, but more-so on what works
in the real world, and how to
effectively perform, or out-perform,
all of the competition.

When it comes down to what
makes a real pick up artist, or any
playboy for that matter, the secret
is just as I will divulge it. The
90-10 rule applies- even though the
game is 90 percent of just being
your own true alpha self, its the
ten percent that counts. These 10%
are what I learned after getting the
girls, and what eventually led to my
picking up the most beautiful women,
women I didn't even know that

flocked to my door.

The Big 3

Have you ever heard the story about the three goats trying to cross over a bridge that has a troll living underneath it? Its a good story and it goes something like a small goat crossed over the bridge, but the troll didn't eat him. A medium sized goat crossed over the bridge, but the troll didn't eat him. And so on the story goes until a big goat tries crossing the troll's bridge and the troll attacks him, but the big goat is strong enough to throw the troll back over the side of the bridge.

Love can be like this to an extent. You might be able to get away with a few little things and you might be able to let others get away with some of the little things, but the big things always get noticed.

If you really want to practice the effects and methods of this book, then you need to realize that a book cannot make up the right conditions necessary for you to get what you want, you have to do this. Nothing in this book is designed to create environments in which you have control- This is what you have to do. You have to go out and do the little things before you can get noticed in a big way. That's what this book is designed to do- Get noticed in a big way!

By getting noticed immediately for your pick up game or your skills with women, you limit yourself to what you'll be able to do when you're really ready. Instead of trying to sleep with women immediately, you need to treat this

like the three Billy goats- start
small and cross each bridge that you
come to, but don't forget to invest
in yourself and any possible
reputation that might come your way
because reputation will be key in
getting strangers to offer you their
sex.

To turn a phrase, "It's
important to always be prepared for
success." The preparation you
receive in this book is not just
tips for you to follow, but actual
ways to delve into the worlds you
want to be in. I say worlds, but
maybe the word 'places' is more apt.
You don't have to go to a bar to

pick up women, or a club. Granted a lot of women who want sex frequent these locals, but you don't need that per say. What you do is your business, but with these methods If you try them recklessly, you might end up with multiple women at one time. So, be careful.

What love?

While it's true that I cannot make this book to make you do anything, it is possible in making this book to use techniques on my end that will enhance the way in which you perform the methods on you end. NLP, hypnosis, self-help; all of these things are great but the most effective technique I have ever learned was taught to me in college as I earned my English degree.

This technique promised that by simple writing, and thus a reader, I would be completely able to tap into the psyche of any individual and communicate with the genetic whole of that person. Imagine by using simple commonalities and archetypes, especially certain doctrines and symbols, that you can communicate over the internet, or by pen and paper, between individuals in a way as complex as any geneticist in the laboratory.

The secret is that time is eternal, and for what that's worth, we all have the cave-man-alpha-male living inside us just as much as we have the star-dwelling-future-man waiting for us. Getting to both of these alternate personas is what's important, as well as getting to the opposite sexes.

To become an instant legend in your town, city, state it is important that you do your own research as well. Just for the reason that you have a chance encounter with another living being that also knows these techniques you should know what's behind your new game. Luckily, the first person to use this game was dead a long time ago, so no one person can actually claim it as their own. Why its been kept a secret for so long is anybody's guess, but I'd put my money on the fact that it not only gets sex from women, but it earns love and trust- by the way of perfect 10 sex.

And that's the 10% from the rule we talked about earlier. Its being the perfect lover. The one the women want so bad they talk about when no guys are around. Just don't

get a complex after it happens to
you, but be ready for one.

     If this sounds interesting to
you, and is something you really
know you want- then just keep
reading!

One-Nighter

"From the first time I saw her
I knew she was going to be mine."
This is what I thought about as he
sat next to her on my couch, in my
apartment. She was right at home
sitting with him on the sofa facing
the T.V. as I played v-jay for over
an hour. I felt like a clown trying
to entertain them just wishing he
would leave, but I needed him to be
there because I couldn't figure out
just how to get her to sleep with
me, and I knew he could sleep with

her that night.

My plan in bringing him here was to get him to loosen up drinking a few beers, while I stayed sober enough to notice how it was that he got so close to her so fast. It worked of course because five minutes after he arrived she was next to him getting closer and closer with him, just giggling like a schoolgirl and laughing every time he said her name.

After an hour of watching them together while I played cool video after video, I started to feel tired. I could have given up like I usually do and just told them to leave. But what good would that of done because if I did that he was sure to sleep with her that night- and that's what I wanted to do. So instead of telling them I was tired and just giving it up and letting her walk off with him I changed gears. I started playing the same videos over and over. I started playing the videos nobody likes- not even me. And before long his game started to give way.

I had introduced a little bit of awkwardness to the room, and their conversation started to give, which is just what I needed for an opening. I took the insults and dirty looks with a grain of salt and started playing the good videos, the ones we hadn't seen yet, but not before I was sitting in front of the two of them with their sole attention now on me.

You see, they had to take a breath before commencing the flirting anymore, mostly to spare each other the embarrassment of what had happened on the T.V. Well I took that opportunity to sit down in front of them and start suggesting some of the videos were really awesome, the ones I played while they were too busy staring into each other's eyes. They had no choice but to agree, and here's why:

They didn't know each other well enough to assume they had so much in common so that they could sit together for an hour and cozy up to one another. They needed me in the background making things look great, playing all the latest and greatest videos of their lives so that they could talk, baby talk. Once I made the videos awkward the two of them had to back up, they were feeling awkward to, so I gave myself the chance to come over and sit right in front of the T.V.

Neither of them cared too much about the T.V. though so they had to just sit and wait for something to come up for them to baby talk about. I didn't give them that chance though, instead I sat there and talked about the videos, and not to him either- but to her. She took every word I said about the videos as good as gold for a number of reasons:

1. She had already gave her opinions on most of them to him, but now she was sitting with me and had to repeat her voice.

2. I knew her better than he

did because I had been listening to her and he had only been trying to use a routine to keep the baby talk going.

3. I played the videos so I knew more about them than he ever could have.

After I began a conversation with the girl the night went much more the way I had wanted it. The only problem was now that I had shut down my drunken friend he was turning into a bit of a problem for me. I couldn't get rid of him just yet because he had turned into the entertainment for the night, now that I was done playing v-j.

He copped an attitude pretty quick, so I had to move him to the kitchen with the beer, while I took his seat at the couch, with her. I knew he would have to regroup and try to gain command of his game before returning, which he did but by that time it was too late. You see, I wasn't drinking so I had my wits and finesse when it came to the physical act I laid on my new girlfriend at the couch. He sat on the floor in front of us, but in a matter of minutes he was on his back beer in hand. I had my arm around her, and suggested we move to the bedroom, which we did- we left him lying there, and I told him to let himself out when he was finished laying there. I scored. Not him.

I took her into the bedroom and the next time I came out of there he was no longer hanging around. He apparently got the point and the next time I spoke with him he wanted to know what had happened to that beautiful girl. He asked this thinking I had let her get away, and thus caused him to miss his big chance with her, but that's not what happened as I explained to him. He couldn't believe it when I told him what did happen and tried to put it off as a fluke in his game, but I know better- I had completely destroyed his tried and proved game, one that he had polished off on every living person he knew. And what did I do- I used a completely unheard of technique that caused this girl to love me, as I will explain in the next sections.

Recap

1. How do you say her name? Does it sound stern and authoritative? Or does it sound friendly and warming? Have you ever heard the pick-up lines that go with

a girl's name? Here are a few you
need to get to know.

-You look like a Cindy?

-Hey have we met, what's your
name again?

-God, J----, I know we just met
but it feels like I have known you
forever, like maybe in a past life,
or something.

Do these sound familiar to you?
They should because they're in the
movies, on T.V., and in all the best
literature. Someone always seems to
make a big deal out of a person's
name, but why? The answer is pretty
simple, its because they have to

build strong rapport with the girl
as fast as possible, and saying her
name is the number one way to do
this. So its true what they say
about it all being in a name. Not
that that means you need to know
everyone's name before you sleep
with them, but only that if you do
chose to use her name you need to be
100% sure you can say it in a
friendly, comfortable manner.

2. Know your stuff. If you are
going to memorize anything that
resembles a routine to pick up
women, don't waste your time. Use
your time wisely and memorize
specific facts and popular nuances,

so that way when you actually do talk to a women she won't feel like you are wasting her time- like so many others.

Example: You hear a song in a public place while standing next to a group. The hottest female in the group says she loves the song. The alpha male of the group has no choice but to say he too also loves the song. You can now feel safe in saying to the group I know this song its "G--", and by telling them the facts you know you become instantly more interesting than them- so much so that they want to be around you.

3. It wasn't so much that I wanted to have the best time that night. I just wanted to sleep with this girl, not that she was anyone in particular, just a girl I wanted to sleep with. I didn't need to be the life of the party or extremely social, I just needed to be driven.

It could have happened the other way around with me letting myself out of my own apartment, but it didn't because I was prepared. I knew exactly what to do and when to do it, so much more than my pick up artist friend whom by the way sticks to the numbers, the game plan, just a little too much for his own good.

Playing by the number is the number one way to lose- and that goes for any situation in life.

Drama 101

If you can get a woman's name and use it correctly, in a warm, confident, and friendly manner you are half way there.

If you can use your own specific knowledge of important and relevant things you can get all the way there.

If Love is what you want, all

you have to do is find it. It should
stick out in the real world, every
opportunity to find Love, it should
be obvious. All you have to do is to
find the thing, this would
preferably be a women, and learn its
name. After that all you have to do
is keep exercising that name on your
tongue and trying it around new and
exciting people and things.

The real secret is in what you
say and how you say it. You don't
need a routine, but if you want to
get good at using names try reading
those books they sell in the grocery
stores that list all the most
popular baby names and what each

name means. This is great exercise
and will pay off the first time
there is a name you recognize and
need to use.

The thing to do in speaking is
to match your partner in tone, in
timing, and in registry. What I mean
is you need to speak at the same
volume as her. You can't be too loud
all the time, its a turn off that
makes it look like you can't hear.
You need to keep your attention
focused on the moment. Girls love
this, and its more fun, so don't try
to act.

Pay attention to her and try to

keep up, if she is ready for sex
that means she's getting excited in
a certain way, you need to feed into
this and if she starts to laugh or
giggle at your jokes then need to
stop joking and laugh a little too
to show her your still paying
attention.

When you talk to her make sure
your talking to her. In the first
few minutes of any conversation I
try to win her over, but as soon as
you see this working you need to
move your speech and attention away
from winning the room to winning
her. Move in close and start to
speak more directly to and about

her, and pay attention- and don't
forget her name.

In order to speak to the woman
inside the woman, which is the woman
you want to speak to, you have to be
the man that women want to be with.
By releasing your inner alpha-male
she must respond in kind, or she's
not worth the time. By using this
method of speech and attention you
are reaching her inner woman, that's
the one that wants you, it'll work
every time if you let it.

Flings

    "This time its going to be different." This is what I thought as I sat at my best friend's house staring at the posters on his wall. This guy always had a way to really create a great atmosphere around his place. I can't even remember what the poster was of but it was something really cool about drinking and women.

    We were sitting around making jokes and sharing stories about girls when I got a call from one of my Ex's friends. She was super- hot and really sweet, so her phone call really got me excited. From what I could tell from her call she was just bored, and since we had never slept together, I was surprised when she wanted me to come over to her place. I was in automatically, but later realized I was only degrading the value of myself by answering to her every whim.

By de-valuing myself I mean I was going in to a set of circumstances that were not prime to pick her up. If we had been somewhere together and she wanted me to leave with her, this would have been fine, but its not what was happening.

I asked my best friend John, owner of the house we were at, if he wanted to go and visit Meg, the girl who called, and her roommate, and he was not into it. I had to do some real convincing, which was easy because talking to my guy friends is simple, so eventually he decided to come along.

At the girls apartment things went downhill fast. No action whatsoever was going down in my department, but John was into the roommate and made his move by going into her bedroom- leaving me alone with Meg. We sat there with hardly anything to say and the awkward silence was stinging. We really had nothing to talk about because we were both in boredom mode, that's why to this day I simply refuse to go on house calls to girls who are just hanging out.

There's a much better way to approach a woman who wants your company, and this way actually leads to sex on behalf of the man daring enough to try. The trick is to get the girl to do something, anything. The basic principle behind this is that she's not just sitting around, but instead has some momentum behind her.

I thought the right move was going to be to get her to her bedroom, but this was a huge mistake. Once we went to her bedroom the only change was that now she was laying on her back talking and I was sitting on the floor, or the corner of the bed, listening to her problems. I was doing better with myself in the living room than I did in the bedroom, but then again the old saying 'out of the frying pan into the fire' was started for a reason.

At this point I couldn't decide
what to do so after listening to her
problems for half an hour I
suggested we see what John was into.
He was waiting for us on the sofa of
the front room, but Meg's roommate
was still lying in bed, apparently
in the same mode as her BFF. This is
when it came to me to try to build
positive momentum and get the girls
excited. I had no help from John
because he had went straight for the
goods back in this girls room, and
when she backed him off he got
characteristically upset and sat his
ass in the living room alone.

I took in John's story with a

little bit of pity because he was a
self-proclaimed pick up artist, who
had great success in the bars and
clubs near his house. I couldn't
feel too sorry for him as he went
into the girl's kitchen and produced
a cold beer from the fridge. He
suggested we all drink a few and
then risk the D.U.I. we might get in
driving back to his place. He
believed that by getting the girls
into his territory he could get them
to do anything he liked.

I thought better of his plan
and suggested that Meg grab her
roommate from her room, before John
tried making his move again. Meg

retrieved her friend and while they both gave John some of the coldest stares I have ever seen as he stood leaning over the kitchen counter drinking his beer. I told John to hang out and finish off a few more beers while I took the ladies for a walk.

It was the change of atmosphere that they needed- no more distress, no more idle minds, no more problems, and no more John. We found a Pair of swing-sets around back of the girls' apartment complex, and we actually enjoyed using them, taking turns pushing each other. When we had finally cleared our minds and

were living in the present, just
enjoying each other's company things
changed on the spot.

We all became less like animal
predators trying to scare each other
off, and we became more intimate
with each other like we really were
friends for life. We went back in to
see where John had ended up, and he
was about a beer away from passing
out on the girl's sofa, he was
drowning in self-pity.

The girls and I hardly even
noticed the slurs that came out of
him as we passed by him to Meg's
bedroom where we could all three of

us spend some time. And that was it-
we brought the positive attitudes
with us into the bedroom and ended
up having sex until 3 in the
morning.

That's right I got the goods
and didn't try any of the patented
pick up artist moves that John
swears by to this day, as he fills
his apartment with trophy after
trophy from his last night's
conquest. I chose to keep my self-
motivated and attentive to the women
around me and now I have no problem
getting sex whenever I want it.

Recap

1. Momentum- You have to have it before sex. Momentum is like Viagra, only its 100% natural. You need a girl to not just be sitting around half the day before she decides to call you for some action. The wrong way to build momentum is to tire the girl out, doing too much. I tired girl isn't a fun girl, unless she's younger than you, because than she likely has more energy than after you wear out.

Good momentum starts like an hour before the prime time to get her to have sex with you. An hour is enough time for you to get ready for work, to get ready for the big game on T.V., or to unwind after dinner. The momentum you need to build does not come from her watching t.v. all day. If she calls you from her sofa wanting to talk or hang out because she's been stuck to the sofa all day and she's tired of reruns, this is not good.

After a woman has a completely lazy day she is full of bad energy, she's just been building up a bad negative ball of emotion all day, and now she wants to share that with you. If she chose you to be the one

to share all her inner turmoil with,
you should definitely reassess the
situation, because that energy
turned to sex is not the kind of sex
you want.

2. Atmosphere is something you
create. Its not something you should
be afraid of, and it is totally
under your control, unlike people.

To really get what it means to
create atmosphere you need to leave
your preconceived notions at the
door. Atmosphere doesn't have to be
preplanned or set up in your living
room, kitchen, or bathroom. It
doesn't exist in a restaurant or in

the club, as a matter of fact it doesn't exist. And running around looking for it is a mistake- only if you can't find it. Its not really inside you, but that's a good guess too.

All it takes to create positive feelings about a place is an open attitude. Its a lot like the saying 'you can't see the forest through the trees." In the same way its like going into a flower garden and after examining every single flower leaving to see the other gardens in the area without, you guessed 'stopping to smell the roses." The secret is to look at the whole and

stay focused on the individual, only
not the individuals that make up the
whole, but the individual you are-
or who your lover is.

3. Keep yourself clean! This
means a lot in the real world. A
clean person is one who does not
allow the clutter in life to fill
his rooms or his mind. I cannot
stress it enough that living in a
way that reflects inner harmony
creates situations in the real world
that are harmonious. Getting angry,
or overly self- confident are two of
the biggest mistakes a pick- up
artist can make. They lead to
trouble and can easily be avoided by

a discriminating person.

What it takes to pick up a beautiful woman is an art, a pick up artist needs to know complete mastery over his actions and his surroundings at all times. This is the only true way to make a women believe they are wanted. You can practice for hours picking up women, but never really understand what it means. If your scoring with the girls its because you have mastered something, but what you master is a part of you- it is you.

Drama 201

So, in order to love a woman,
or to be her lover, what it really
takes is for you to first love
yourself. I hear people all the time
telling me that they can't love
themselves, but then turn around and
pick up a woman that feels the same
way about themselves. If you really
want to hear something messed up
then listen to this. The man who
picks up the girl that is like him
is locked into that relationship,
and they deserve each other.

The art of the pick up is to
pick- up the girls that are out of
your league, or at least the ones

you believe to be so. It takes a real dummy to not see that he has learned the wrong material after his relationships end one after another after another. You need to realize that by being a better person you really are offering what every woman wants. You are tapping into the psyche of all women when you become a pick up artist with skills.

By letting women revolve around you and your plans of action you are in essence inviting women to sleep with you, just for fun. And women love to do this as long as there is no detriment to their selves. The way to ensure no harm is done is to

tap deep into her inner desire for
an alpha male, and then to create
the environment in which you are
that male.

When you do this to a woman the
woman automatically senses that
there are no real strings attached
outside of the agreement that you
share together. And there isn't
either, its all it takes. Be the
real world player with class, and
create worlds in which her psyche
can find fulfillment then you will
receive sexual fulfillment together.
Its kind of like visiting a fantasy
suite in a hotel- without paying the
bill.

You are the only one that can create this magic world for her, and she will come to you for it. Not only that but remember how I promised that women that are complete strangers to you will flock to you, well this is why, and this is a powerful technique almost entirely overlooked by 99% of pick up artists too busy with their selves and their conquests back at the super social bar or club.

Relationships

"Sometimes I wish there were three of me." This is what I sometimes think about, but I'm pretty sure a lot of the time that three wouldn't be enough of me. Realistically though one is enough of me, just so long as I can pick up beautiful women, whom will do most of the work.

The first time I met Josie I was working my ass off as usual trying to work my way through college. She was gorgeous and tall, she was it. I had been working at this place near my college campus for almost a year when she got on and I found out she was trying to do the same thing.

I was top of my class at school, but that didn't get me any breaks at work. I worked hard every day with some real work-ethic (that is until Josie started working with me.) I immediately saw the attention she received at work, and I knew that if I landed her with some quality pick up material I could make life a lot easier for the both of us.

The key to working with her was that no matter what she did she always got a break, this included time to talk to guys and boyfriends while she was on the clock. I never got away with slacking off on the clock, so I figured with a little effort I get Josie back to work, only now she'd be doing most of my work.

The boss didn't care what she did, she was too good looking, and I began to talk to her and show her the ropes at work. Giving her the impression that my job was great and that I was really good at it, and hard-working, was easy because all I had to do was watch out for her to start to slack off and talk to other guys and then I would immediately concentrate on whatever it was I was doing only way more hardcore than the task required.

By my concentrating on what I was doing I was actually giving off the impression that I was having more fun than anyone else. The next time I spoke to Josie, and she was slacking off a little before the end of the day, all I had to do was ask her for a little help at what I was doing to get out of there. She liked talking to me already, and now she had a reason to get physical, which is a good thing- Kino!

Anyway, those late night work sessions escalated pretty quickly and before long she was coming home with me and we were having great sex! The effort I put into showing her things at work paid off double when she now used her spare time at work in doing the tasks I hated doing, and she almost never spoke to other guys anymore because she was too busy.

The first time I met Ness I was stunned. She was the average sorority girl, but in most of my classes sorority life was the biggest secret since Socrates. She was smart and beautiful, but she was way to quiet. None of the guys in our classes at the college new how to approach her, so she seemed very untouchable.

The only reason she even knew I existed was I was very vocal in my classes and I liked to help other classmates when I had a chance. Ness didn't need help though because she was straight A material, the only way to approach her was to wait, which is a strong point of mine- patience.

After our classes really

started to move along in the
materials we were responsible for I
didn't have much time to fantasize
about what it would be like to pick
up on Ness, so I did what I did
best- I focused on the task at hand,
which happened to be getting an
insane amount of paperwork turned
in.

I needed a way to get the
smartest and prettiest girl in class
to liven up a bit so these classes
would be bearable, so I decided to
put in some extra time after class.
Gathering my papers and hanging
around after class was dismissed was
a good move because it reminded me

that I wasn't the only one falling
behind.

I quickly moved this taking of
a few extra minutes after class to
my creating an encounter with Ness.
She never hung around after class,
but at least I could see which way
she was going. I approached her in
the same fashion as most beautiful
women and didn't even give her a
chance to act shy. I used my efforts
to make myself look like the cool
kid come apart. I shuffled papers as
I walked next to her, but as soon as
she noticed this I cut the act and
concentrated my effort, which had
the effect of quickly assembling my

papers while moving at her pace, side- by- side with her step. I came together in front of her and she was amazed; she saw what she wanted but never took the time to ask for- me.

It was a long walk that day, but it was nice and sunny outside, so taking her time Ness was relaxed as she walked with me. Before long she had opened up about her life and studies. I used this opportunity not only to sleep with the hottest girl in any of my classes, but also my grades improved as soon as Ness was doing most of the homework.

She never questioned doing my

classwork because she knew that I
was way too focused on my degree to
risk anything crazy. I used
concentrated effort to show her it
was ok to help, and thus be helped-
only I helped her sexually.

From that day on I walked home
with her and she was doing half of
the research I hadn't had time for,
but I found the time for her.
Concentrated effort sounds so boring
and difficult but its really no
different than multi-tasking.

Recap
1. Effort- you got to really be

there in the moment to know what you are doing. Confidence is a direct result of sustained effort, and confidence attracts attention, especially from women. The saying about 'try, try again." Wasn't meant for losers, it was meant for those people that want more confidence in their daily lives.

Effort is like the moving sky. Sounds strange but hear me out. Effort can't really be trapped up in a bottle, or judged- unless you're referring to energy, but I'm not. What you do with yourself at any given time is what is considered effort. If you put effort into your home life, it gets better at home. If you put effort into your social life, it gets better. So effort isn't any certain thing at all, its just what you do with yourself.

2. Concentration is easier than it sounds. It doesn't have to be like the child's game where you remember pictures. In fact concentration is better left to the individual. It speaks volumes about ones' character, which is another good thing that women love. Showing focus on a task, concentrating, shows that you are the caring sort of person, the person other people want to be around. And no matter how

many times you lose your
concentration you can easily get it
back with a little effort just doing
what you always do- do work!

I need to stress again that
concentrating is not hard. It does
not mean you are remembering facts
and trying to recall them with
amazing accuracy, as some would
define it. But more than that
concentrating is the act of slowing
down your actions and relying solely
on past and learned events and
outcomes of a specific function or
whole of that specific act. Sounds
complicated but its really not, as
I'll explain below in the 3 part of

this section.

3. An act of love can be defined by its outcome; if it is an act of love than its result must be a desirable one. You go to the store to buy a t-shirt; you find a shirt you think you really love it, so you buy it. Story ends when you wear that shirt and you feel love: for the shirt, for your buying it, and for everyone who sees you in it because its so cool.

Love should be like a brand, a certain label of fashion. If you were to go out shopping and always but the same label of clothing you

would be a model of love. Not only
that, but every time you go out as
the pick up artist and your wearing
your love label, you are essentially
letting other people identify with
you. Love is never impaired by love
itself. You should be wearing a
label you love, so that when your
life as a pick up artist really
picks up momentum you will be
identified as a player with game.
Sentiment is fashionable, and women
will know before and after that you
are open for sex if they want it.

Drama 301

Its easy to see how this technique can be easily applied to the pick up artist, and so it should be. Because you have the right to be happy you should never feel bad about your methods. People do these things all the time with zero awareness of what they're doing, so do you but now you can easily apply your time to picking up girls.

Guidelines for this behavior are so minimal they're hardly worth mentioning, but here goes anyway.

-In life a lot of times, especially in the life of a pick up artist, its dog eat dog- as the saying goes. Being the alpha male sometimes means taking things that weren't initially intended for your pleasure. Saying this is easy but keeping it unproven is another matter altogether.

Just because you meet a beautiful woman in a perfect situation doesn't mean that she's completely available to you. That's your job in figuring out just who she is, and how available you can get her to be.

The nonsense of it all is that most men before they become pick up artists are aware of the rejection factor. Well I'm here to tell you not to give any mind to this type of thinking. A rejection from a woman simply means that you are not completely giving her the 'go' to please you. Believe it or not you've got the alpha male in you- its just bigger than you want to admit at times.

You are accessing the girl's desire to please you, and by doing so you are accessing her inner alpha female- that's the way that a woman pleases a man. If you give her any doubt about the situation she doesn't know any better than to trust your instinct- that's how females live. Trust yourself to make responsible decisions and the women will trust you as well.

Therefor a rejection is really just your way of telling a girl that sex could be a mistake at this point, this is why sometimes its just better for the pick-up artist to go for a kiss or even a phone number. You already know this - I'm moving on.

Well...

Now you know. You know the secrets to becoming a perfect lover. Its so simple is crazy, but so is love. There is nothing you can't do by following the instructions contained in this book, and there likely won't be any changing this for some time. The stuff that matters is in having fun while you become not just another pick up artist. Bad attitudes don't make this stuff not work, bad attitudes just make this life different. You can in theory be the worst person, and still get away with being the best possible lover, I've seen it before. What counts is that you are capable of being different and still able to apply this material.

Everyone is different, and I don't expect anyone to be just like me, or to use these methods as I did. You can just do it your way, but the principles of it will still be available to you, no matter what your like or what you're in to. This book is made to transcend race lines, cross borders, be timeless, and its best to follow any information contained within this book with your gut.

Don't forget that living with game means living to its fullest, which means you can't skip out on the other facets of your life. If you start to think that life is just a game than your game will fall apart. You have to understand that the methods, techniques, and results of the pick-up artist are so real that everyone needs to try them once in life just to be fully alive- its human nature.

AIL
As you try more and more of the

techniques herein you may find
yourself looking for more
information, so if that becomes the
case the best advice I can give is
that I have also written a short
series of novels that, while they
are not instructional in nature as
this material is, they are formatted
to be essential living tools. By
living tools I mean that the
characters and situations contained
in the novels are not to be found
elsewhere in any other media you may
come across. These novels are unique
and completely distinct from the
secular culture in which the average
pick up artist was raised and now

thrives, so if you feel the need then go ahead and try them out.

The series name is "An Impaired Love" and can be found online. The materials within them are construed to develop habits exactly similar to the instructional tips found here, but they are formatted to read just as if you were involved in reading any story. Albeit, in writing these novels I put my best foot forward and designed them to have positive lasting impact in the readers' life, often without any cognizance on the readers part. They're just made for the little voice of conscience that is said to exist. The precept behind

them is entirely revolutionary, much
like the think and blink tactics of
this book, but its harder to explain
how to write a novel that is
intended to be read as a manual than
I care to admit.

There are doubtless other, and
by point of view better, books on
PUAs, but the other books by the
more professional artists out there
have not one single gain on you than
you already have- except experience,
which this book is full of to the
top. The methods are the same to a
degree, its just up to you to find
your own program and to work it from
there- this is just to get you

moving remember!

Why love works!

Love works in mysterious ways. Have you ever heard that? Well it's true, but what does it mean. To me it has always meant that love works where the eyes can't see. Before you close your eyes and wait for love though, I'd like to offer these alternative approaches:

Love comes when least expected.

Love is a battlefield.

Love is never impaired by love.

It's the third option that I

want to focus on- Love is never impaired by love.

For this to be true that must mean that love, any love, is just as strong as the next. The girl of your dreams, if this holds true, might just as well be replaced by the girl next door. The key is your letting it happen. Allowing love to open fully and explain the secrets of your heart is no easy trick, but with patients it can happen.

I'm not really a mushy or completely over-sensitive person, I'm actually quite aggressive, which is something I'm working on especially in staying patient. But the point is, that love works on whoever it wants in its own special way. There is no love potion, no secret recipe that is all defining. Only are there different ways of viewing the world. If you want to see the world one way, than do it, but it's essential for good game, or being the perfect lover, that you are able to shift gears, or may I call it being open to change.

The only material not presented in this book, in order to keep to its short format and length are on everyday living. But you're already a living breathing person who

understands the problems that men
and women face in the world today,
so I have decided to leave out my
own personal experiences.

Accurate portrayal of true love
is more difficult than I ever
imagined, it's just out there.

www.ingramcontent.com/pod-product-compliance
Lightning Source LLC
Chambersburg PA
CBHW070621130626
46556CB00001B/434